Corner House Publishers

SOCIAL SCIENCE REPRINTS

❦   ❦   ❦

General Editor MAURICE FILLER

EDITOR'S PREFACE

❦ ❦ ❦

ON November 21, 1852, ten-year old Carolyn
Richards of Canandaiga, New York made the
first entry in a journal that was to cover a twenty
year period in the history of this country. From
her opening lines—"I am ten years old today, and
I think I will write a journal and tell who I am
and what I am doing."—to her closing entry on
November 21, 1872, we are treated to a fascinating picture of rural life in 19th century America.
Carolyn Richards was a highly intelligent and
perceptive young lady. Her observations and
comments on life in Canandaiga give us an inti-
mate view of adolescence and maturity in Victor-
ian America such as no text on social history can
remotely provide.

Some excerpts: December 20, 1855,—"Susan
B. Anthony is in town and spoke in Bemis Hall
this afternoon. She had a large audience and she
talked very plainly about our rights and how we
ought to stand up for them... She asked us all
to come up and sign our names ... A whole lot
of us went up and signed the paper."

April 15, 1861,—"The storm has broken upon
us. The Confederates fired on Fort Sumter ...

President Lincoln has issued a call for 75,000 men and many are volunteering to go all around us. How strange and awful it seems."

May, 1861,—"A lot of us girls went down to the train and took flowers to the soldiers as they were passing through and they cut buttons from their coats and gave to us as souvenirs."

July 4, 1863,—"The terrible battle of Gettysburg brings to Canandaiga sad news of our soldier boys of the 126th Regiment."

Monday Morning, April 10.—"Lee has surrendered! and all the people seem crazy in consequence. The bells are ringing, boys and girls, men and women are running through the streets wild with excitement. . ."

School life, church life, home life, social life—all are presented with a charm, a grace, a sense of humor that carry the reader straight into the life of the times.

Carolyn Richards has provided us through her diary a document of great interest and inestimable value to the social historian, the student, the general reader interested in how life was lived in small town America one hundred years ago.

"From the first page to the last my attention was riveted. To call it fascinating barely expresses the quality of the charm." Margaret E. Sangster, Introduction.

Caroline Cowles Richards
(From a daguerreotype taken in 1860)

VILLAGE LIFE IN AMERICA

1852–1872

INCLUDING THE PERIOD OF THE
AMERICAN CIVIL WAR AS TOLD IN
THE DIARY OF A SCHOOL-GIRL

By

CAROLINE COWLES RICHARDS *Clarke*

WITH AN INTRODUCTION
BY
MARGARET E. SANGSTER

NEW AND ENLARGED EDITION

CORNER HOUSE PUBLISHERS
WILLIAMSTOWN, MASSACHUSETTS 01267
1972

To

My dear brothers,

JAMES AND JOHN,

who, by precept and example,

have encouraged me,

and to my beloved sister,

ANNA,

whose faith and affection

have been my chief inspiration,

this little volume

is lovingly inscribed.

Naples, N. Y.

CONTENTS

CONTENTS

LIST OF ILLUSTRATIONS

PUBLISHERS' NOTE

After this book was in type, on March 29, 1913, the author, Mrs. Caroline Richards Clarke, died at Naples, New York.

INTRODUCTION

THE Diary of Caroline Cowles Richards fell into my hands, so to speak, out of space. I had no previous acquaintance with the author, and I sat down to read the book one evening in no especial mood of anticipation. From the first page to the last my attention was riveted. To call it fascinating barely expresses the quality of the charm. Caroline Richards and her sister Anna, having early lost their mother, were sent to the home of her parents in Canandaigua, New York, where they were brought up in the simplicity and sweetness of a refined household, amid Puritan traditions. The children were allowed to grow as plants do, absorbing vitality from the atmosphere around them. Whatever there was of gracious formality in the manners of aristocratic people of the period, came to them as their birthright, while the spirit of the truest democracy pervaded their home. Of this Diary it is not too much to say that it is a revelation of childhood in ideal conditions.

The Diary begins in 1852, and is continued until 1872. Those of us who lived in the latter half of the nineteenth century recall the swift transitions, the rapid march of science and various changes in social customs, and as we meet allusions to these in the leaves of the girl's Diary we live our past over again with peculiar pleasure.

Far more has been told us concerning the South during the Civil War than concerning the North. Fiction has found the North a less romantic field, and the South has been chosen as the background of many a stirring novel, while only here and there has an author been found who has known the deep-hearted loyalty of the Northern States and woven the story into narrative form. The girl who grew up in Canandaigua was intensely patriotic, and from day to day vividly chronicled what she saw, felt, and heard. Her Diary is a faithful record of impressions of that stormy time in which the nation underwent a baptism of fire. The realism of her paragraphs is unsurpassed.

Beyond the personal claim of the Diary and the certainty to give pleasure to a host of readers, the author appeals to Americans in general because of her family and her friends. Her father and grandfather were Presbyterian ministers. Her Grandfather Richards was for twenty years President of Auburn Theological Seminary. Her brother, John Morgan Richards of London, has recently given to the world the Life and Letters of his gifted and lamented daughter, Pearl Mary-Terèse Craigie, known best as John Oliver Hobbes. The famous Field brothers and their father, Rev. David Dudley Field, and their nephew, Justice David J. Brewer, of the United States Supreme Court, were her kins-men. Miss Hannah Upham, a distinguished teacher mentioned in the Diary, belongs to the group of American women to whom we owe the initiative of what we now choose to call the higher education of the sex. She, in common with Mary Lyon, Emma Willard, and Eliza Bayliss Wheaton, gave a forward impulse to the liberal education of women, and our privilege is to keep their memory green. They are to be remembered by what they have done and by the tender reminiscences found here and there like pressed flowers in a herbarium, in such pages as these.

Miss Richards' marriage to Mr. Edmund C. Clarke occurred in 1866. Mr. Clarke is a veteran of the Civil War and a Commander in the Grand Army of the Republic. His brother, Noah T. Clarke, was the Principal of Canandaigua Academy for the long term of forty years. The dignified, amusing and remarkable personages who were Mrs. Clarke's contemporaries, teachers, or friends are pictured in her Diary just as they were, so that we meet them on the street, in the drawing-room, in church, at prayer-meeting, anywhere and every-where, and grasp their hands as if we, too, were in their presence.

Wherever this little book shall go it will carry good cheer. Fun and humor sparkle through the story of this childhood and girlhood so that the reader will be cheated of ennui, and the sallies of the little sister will provoke mirth and laughter to brighten dull days.   I have read thousands of books. I have never read one which has given me more delight than this.

MARGARET E. SANGSTER.

GLEN RIDGE, NEW JERSEY,
    June, 1911.

THE VILLAGES

CANANDAIGUA, NEW YORK.—A beautiful village, the county seat of Ontario County, situated at the foot of Canandaigua Lake, which is called "the gem of the inland lakes" of Western New York, about 325 miles from New York city.

NAPLES, NEW YORK.—A small village at the head of Canandaigua Lake, famous for its vine-clad hills and unrivaled scenery.

GENEVA, NEW YORK.—A beautiful town about 16 miles from Canandaigua.

EAST BLOOMFIELD, NEW YORK.—An ideal farming region and suburban village about 8 miles from Canandaigua.

PENN YAN, NEW YORK.—The county seat of Yates County, a grape center upon beautiful Lake Keuka.

ROCHESTER, NEW YORK.—A flourishing manufacturing city, growing rapidly, less than 30 miles from Canandaigua, and 120 miles from Niagara Falls.

AUBURN, NEW YORK.—Noted for its Theological Seminary, nearly one hundred years old, and for being the home of William H. Seward and other American Statesmen.

THE VILLAGERS

Mʀ. ᴀɴᴅ Mʀs. THOMAS BEALS, Grandfather and Grandmother

CAROLINE ᴀɴᴅ ANNA } Grandchildren of Mr. and
JAMES ᴀɴᴅ JOHN RICHARDS } Mrs. Beals

"AUNT ANN" . . .
"AUNT MARY" CARR .
"AUNT GLORIANNA" . } Sons and daughters of
"UNCLE HENRY" . . } Mr. and Mrs. Beals
"UNCLE THOMAS" . .

Rᴇᴠ. O. E. DAGGETT, D.D. Pastor of Canandaigua Congregational Church

NOAH T. CLARKE . . Principal Canandaigua Academy for Boys

Hoɴ. FRANCIS GRANGER . Postmaster-General,U.S.A.

Gᴇɴᴇʀᴀʟ JOHN A. GRANGER Of New York State Militia

GIDEON GRANGER . . Son of Hon. Francis

ALBERT GRANGER . . Son of General Granger

JOHN GREIG . . . . Wealthy Scotsman long time resident of Canandaigua

MYRON H. CLARK . . Governor, State of New York

JUDGE H. W. TAYLOR . Prominent lawyer and jurist

E. M. MORSE . . . . A leading lawyer in Canandaigua

Mɪss ZILPHA CLARKE . School teacher of note

Mɪss CAROLINE CHESEBRO } Well-known writers
Mʀs. GEORGE WILLSON . }

Mɪss HANNAH UPHAM . Eminent instructress and lady principal of Ontario Female Seminary

Mʀ. FRED THOMPSON . Prominent resident, married Miss Mary Clark, daughter of Governor Myron H. Clark.

xiv

School Boys

WILLIAM T. SCHLEY . .
HORACE M. FINLEY . .
ALBERT MURRAY . .
S. GURNEY LAPHAM . . Residing with parents in
CHARLES COY . . . Canandaigua
ELLSWORTH DAGGETT .
CHARLIE PADDOCK . .
MERRITT C. WILLCOX .

WILLIAM H. ADAMS . .
GEORGE N. WILLIAMS . Law Students

WILLIS P. FISKE . . .
EDMUND C. CLARKE . . Teachers in Academy

School Girls

LOUISA FIELD . . .
MARY WHEELER . . .
EMMA WHEELER . . .
LAURA CHAPIN . . .
JULIA PHELPS . . .
MARY PAUL . . . .
BESSIE SEYMOUR . . .
LUCILLA FIELD . . .
MARY FIELD . . . .
ABBIE CLARK . . . Residing with parents in
SUSIE DAGGETT . . . Canandaigua
FRANKIE RICHARDSON .
FANNY GAYLORD . . .
MARY COY . . . .
HELEN COY . . . .
HATTIE PADDOCK . .
SARAH ANTES . . .
LOTTIE LAPHAM . . .
CLARA WILSON . . .
FANNIE PALMER . . .
RITIE TYLER . . . .

VILLAGE LIFE IN AMERICA

1852

November 21, 1852.—I am ten years old to-day, and I think I will write a journal and tell who I am and what I am doing. I have lived with my Grandfather and Grandmother Beals ever since I was seven years old, and Anna, too, since she was four. Our brothers, James and John, came too, but they are at East Bloomfield at Mr. Stephen Clark's Academy. Miss Laura Clark of Naples is their teacher.

Anna and I go to school at District No. 11. Mr. James C. Cross is our teacher, and some of the scholars say he is cross by name and cross by nature, but I like him. He gave me a book by the name of "Noble Deeds of American Women," for reward of merit, in my reading class. To-day, a nice old gentleman, by the name of Mr. William Wood, visited our school. He is Mrs. Nat Gorham's uncle, and Wood Street is named for him. He had a beautiful pear in his hand and said he would give it to the boy or girl who could spell "virgaloo," for that was the name of the pear. I spelt it that way, but it was not right. A little boy, named

William Schley, spelt it right and he got the pear.
I wish I had, but I can't even remember now how
he spelt it. If the pear was as hard as the name I
don't believe any one would want it, but I don't see
how they happened to give such a hard name to
such a nice pear. Grandfather says perhaps Mr.
Wood will bring in a Seckle pear some day, so I
had better be ready for him.

Grandmother told us such a nice story to-day I
am going to write it down in my journal. I think
I shall write a book some day. Miss Caroline
Chesebro did, and I don't see why I can't. If I do,
I shall put this story in it. It is a true story and
better than any I found in three story books
Grandmother gave us to read this week, " Peep of
Day," " Line Upon Line," and " Precept Upon Precept," but this story was better than them all. One
night Grandfather was locking the front door at
nine o'clock and he heard a queer sound, like a baby
crying. So he unlocked the door and found a
bandbox on the stoop, and the cry seemed to come
from inside of it. So he took it up and brought it
into the dining-room and called the two girls, who
had just gone upstairs to bed. They came right
down and opened the box, and there was a poor
little girl baby, crying as hard as could be. They
took it out and rocked it and sung to it and got
some milk and fed it and then sat up all night
with it, by the fire. There was a paper pinned on
the baby's dress with her name on it, " Lily T.

LaMott," and a piece of poetry called " Pity the Poor Orphan." The next morning, Grandfather went to the overseer of the poor and he said it should be taken to the county house, so our hired man got the horse and buggy, and one of the girls carried the baby and they took it away. There was a piece in the paper about it, and Grandmother pasted it into her " Jay's Morning and Evening Exercises," and showed it to us. It said, " A Deposit After Banking Hours." " Two suspicious looking females were seen about town in the afternoon, one of them carrying an infant. They took a train early in the morning without the child. They probably secreted themselves in Mr. Beals' yard and if he had not taken the box in they would have carried it somewhere else." When Grandfather told the clerks in the bank about it next morning, Mr. Bunnell, who lives over by Mr. Daggett's, on the park, said, if it had been left at some people's houses it would not have been sent away. Grandmother says they heard that the baby was adopted afterwards by some nice people in Geneva. People must think this is a nice place for children, for they had eleven of their own before we came. Mrs. McCoe was here to call this afternoon and she looked at us and said: " It must be a great responsibility, Mrs. Beals." Grandmother said she thought " her strength would be equal to her day." That is one of her favorite verses. She said Mrs. McCoe never had any children of her own and perhaps that is the reason she looks so sad at us. Perhaps some one will leave a bandbox and a baby at her door some dark night.

Saturday.—Our brother John drove over from East Bloomfield to-day to see us and brought Julia Smedley with him, who is just my age. John lives at Mr. Ferdinand Beebe's and goes to school and Julia is Mr. Beebe's niece. They make quantities of maple sugar out there and they brought us a dozen little cakes. They were splendid. I offered John one and he said he would rather throw it over the fence than to eat it. I can't understand that. Anna had the faceache to-day and I told her that I would be the doctor and make her a ginger poultice. I thought I did it exactly right but when I put it on her face she shivered and said: "Carrie, you make lovely poultices only they are so cold." I suppose I ought to have warmed it.

Tuesday.—Grandfather took us to ride this afternoon and let us ask Bessie Seymour to go with us. We rode on the plank road to Chapinville and had to pay 2 cents at the toll gate, both ways. We met a good many people and Grandfather bowed to them and said, "How do you do, neighbor?"

We asked him what their names were and he said he did not know. We went to see Mr. Munson, who runs the mill at Chapinville. He took us through the mill and let us get weighed and took

us over to his house and out into the barn-yard to
see the pigs and chickens and we also saw a colt
which was one day old. Anna just wrote in her
journal that " it was a very amusing site."

Sunday.—Rev. Mr. Kendall, of East Bloomfield,
preached to-day. His text was from Job 26, 14:
" Lo these are parts of his ways, but how little a
portion is heard of him." I could not make out
what he meant. He is James' and John's minister.

Wednesday.—Captain Menteith was at our house
to dinner to-day and he tried to make Anna and me
laugh by snapping his snuff-box under the table.
He is a very jolly man, I think.

Thursday.—Father and Uncle Edward Richards
came to see us yesterday and took us down to Mr.
Corson's store and told us we could have anything
we wanted. So we asked for several kinds of
candy, stick candy and lemon drops and bulls' eyes,
and then they got us two rubber balls and two jumping ropes with handles and two hoops and sticks to
roll them with and two red carnelian rings and two
bracelets. We enjoyed getting them very much,
and expect to have lots of fun. They went out to
East Bloomfield to see James and John, and father
is going to take them to New Orleans. We hate
to have them go.

Friday.—We asked Grandmother if we could have some hoop skirts like the seminary girls and she said no, we were not old enough. When we were downtown Anna bought a reed for 10 cents and ran it into the hem of her underskirt and says she is going to wear it to school to-morrow. I think Grandmother will laugh out loud for once, when she sees it, but I don't think Anna will wear it to school or anywhere else. She wouldn't want to if she knew how terrible it looked.

I threaded a dozen needles on a spool of thread for Grandmother, before I went to school, so that she could slip them along and use them as she needed them. She says it is a great help.

Grandmother says I will have a great deal to answer for, because Anna looks up to me so and tries to do everything that I do and thinks whatever I say is "gospel truth." The other day the girls at school were disputing with her about something and she said, "It is so, if it ain't so, for Calline said so." I shall have to "toe the mark," as Grandfather says, if she keeps watch of me all the time and walks in my footsteps.

We asked Grandmother this evening if we could sit out in the kitchen with Bridget and Hannah and the hired man, Thomas Holleran. She said we could take turns and each stay ten minutes by the clock. It gave us a little change. I read once that "variety is the spice of life." They sit around the table and each one has a candle, and Thomas reads

aloud to the girls while they sew. He and Bridget
are Catholics, but Hannah is a member of our
Church. The girls have lived here always, I think,
but I don't know for sure, as I have not lived here
always myself, but we have to get a new hired man
sometimes. Grandmother says if you are as good
to your girls as you are to yourself they will stay a
long time. I am sure that is Grandmother's rule.
Mrs. McCarty, who lives on Brook Street (some
people call it Cat Alley but Grandmother says that is
not proper), washes for us Mondays, and Grandmother always has a lunch for her at eleven o'clock
and goes out herself to see that she sits down and
eats it. Mrs. McCarty told us Monday that Mrs.
Brockle's niece was dead, who lives next door to her.
Grandmother sent us over with some things for their
comfort and told us to say that we were sorry they
were in trouble. We went and when we came back
Anna told Grandmother that I said, " Never mind,
Mrs. Brockle, some day we will all be dead." I am
sure that I said something better than that.

Wednesday.—Mr. Cross had us speak pieces to-
day. He calls our names, and we walk on to the
platform and toe the mark and make a bow and
say what we have got to say. He did not know
what our pieces were going to be and some of them
said the same ones. Two boys spoke: " The boy
stood on the burning deck, whence all but him had
fled." William Schley was one, and he spoke his

the best. When he said, " The flames that lit the battle wreck shone round him o'er the dead," we could almost see the fire, and when he said, " My father, must I stay? " we felt like telling him, no, he needn't. He is going to make a good speaker. Mr. Cross said so. Albert Murray spoke " Excelsior," and Horace Finley spoke nice, too. My piece was, " Why, Phoebe, are you come so soon? Where are your berries, child? " Emma Van Arsdale spoke the same one. We find them all in our reader. Sometime I am going to speak, " How does the water come down at Ladore? " Splashing and flashing and dashing and clashing and all that—it rhymes, so it is easy to remember.

We played snap the whip at recess to-day and I was on the end and was snapped off against the fence. It hurt me so, that Anna cried. It is not a very good game for girls, especially for the one on the end.

Tuesday.—I could not keep a journal for two weeks, because Grandfather and Grandmother have been very sick and we were afraid something dreadful was going to happen. We are so glad that they are well again. Grandmother was sick upstairs and Grandfather in the bedroom downstairs, and we carried messages back and forth for them. Dr. Carr and Aunt Mary came over twice every day and said they had the influenza and the inflammation of the lungs. It was lonesome for us to sit

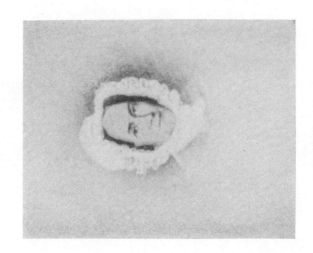

Grandmother Beals

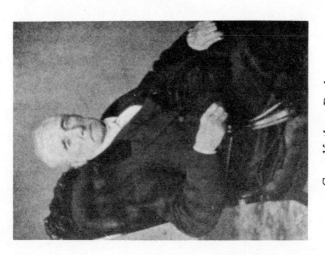

Grandfather Beals

down to the table and just have Hannah wait on us.
We did not have any blessing because there was no
one to ask it.   Anna said she could, but I was afraid
she would not say it right, so I told her she needn't.
We had such lumps in our throats we could not eat
much and we cried ourselves to sleep two or three
nights.   Aunt Ann Field took us home with her one
afternoon to stay all night.   We liked the idea and
Mary and Louisa and Anna and I planned what we
would play in the evening, but just as it was dark our
hired man, Patrick McCarty, drove over after us.
He said Grandfather and Grandmother could not get
to sleep till they saw the children and bid them good-
night.   So we rode home with him.   We never
stayed anywhere away from home all night that we
can remember.   When Grandmother came downstairs the first time she was too weak to walk, so
she sat on each step till she got down.   When
Grandfather saw her, he smiled and said to us:
" When she will, she will, you may depend on't;
and when she won't she won't, and that's the
end on't."   But we knew all the time that he was
very glad to see her.

Sunday, March 20.—It snowed so, that we could not go to church to-day and it was the longest day I ever spent. The only excitement was seeing the snowplow drawn by two horses, go up on this side of the street and down on the other. Grandfather put on his long cloak with a cape, which he wears in real cold weather, and went. We wanted to pull some long stockings over our shoes and go too but Grandmother did not think it was best. She gave us the "Dairyman's Daughter" and "Jane the Young Cottager," by Leigh Richmond, to read. I don't see how they happened to be so awfully good. Anna says they died of "early piety," but she did not say it very loud. Grandmother said she would give me 10 cents if I would learn the verses in the New England Primer that John Rogers left for his wife and nine small children and one at the breast, when he was burned at the stake, at Smithfield, England, in 1555. One verse is, " I leave you here a little book for you to look upon that you may see your father's face when he is dead and gone." It is a very long piece but I got it. Grandmother says " the blood of the martyrs is the seed of the church." Anna learned

" In Adam's fall we sinned all.
My Book and heart shall never part.
The Cat doth play and after slay.
The Dog doth bite a thief at night."

When she came to the end of it and said,

" Zaccheus he, did climb a tree, his Lord to see."

she said she heard some one say, " The tree broke
down and let him fall and he did not see his Lord
at all." Grandmother said it was very wicked indeed and she hoped Anna would try and forget it.

April 1.—Grandmother sent me up into the little
chamber to-day to straighten things and get the
room ready to be cleaned. I found a little book
called " Child's Pilgrim Progress, Illustrated," that
I had never seen before. I got as far as Giant
Despair when Anna came up and said Grandmother
sent her to see what I was doing, and she went
back and told her that I was sitting on the floor in
the midst of books and papers and was so absorbed
in " Pilgrim's Progress " that I had made none myself. It must be a good book for Grandmother did
not say a word. Father sent us " Gulliver's Trav-
els " and there is a gilt picture on the green cover,
of a giant with legs astride and little Lilliputians
standing underneath, who do not come up to his
knees. Grandmother did not like the picture, so

she pasted a piece of pink calico over it, so we could only see the giant from his waist up. I love the story of Cinderella and the poem, " 'Twas the night before Christmas," and I am sorry that there are no fairies and no Santa Claus.

We go to school to Miss Zilpha Clark in her own house on Gibson Street. Other girls who go are Laura Chapin, Julia Phelps, Mary Paul, Bessie Seymour, Lucilla and Mary Field, Louisa Benjamin, Nannie Corson, Kittie Marshall, Abbie Clark and several other girls. I like Abbie Clark the best of all the girls in school excepting of course my sister Anna.

Before I go to school every morning I read three chapters in the Bible. I read three every day and five on Sunday and that takes me through the Bible in a year. Those I read this morning were the first, second and third chapters of Job. The first was about Eliphaz reproveth Job; second, Benefit of God's correction; third, Job justifieth his complaint. I then learned a text to say at school. I went to school at quarter to nine and recited my text and we had prayers and then proceeded with the business of the day. Just before school was out, we recited in " Science of Things Familiar," and in Dictionary, and then we had calisthenics.

We go through a great many figures and sing " A Life on the Ocean Wave," " What Fairy-like Music Steals Over the Sea," " Lightly Row, Lightly Row, O'er the Glassy Waves We Go," and " O Come,

Come Away," and other songs.   Mrs. Judge Taylor wrote one song on purpose for us.

May 1.—I arose this morning about the usual time and read my three chapters in the Bible and had time for a walk in the garden before breakfast. The polyanthuses are just beginning to blossom and they border all the walk up and down the garden. I went to school at quarter of nine, but did not get along very well because we played too much. We had two new scholars to-day, Miss Archibald and Miss Andrews, the former about seventeen and the latter about fifteen.   In the afternoon old Mrs. Kinney made us a visit, but she did not stay very long. In dictionary class I got up sixth, although I had not studied my lesson very much.

July.—Hiram Goodrich, who lives at Mr. Myron H. Clark's, and George and Wirt Wheeler ran away on Sunday to seek their fortunes.   When they did not come back every one was frightened and started out to find them.   They set out right after Sunday School, taking their pennies which had been given them for the contribution, and were gone several days.   They were finally found at Palmyra.   When asked why they had run away, one replied that he thought it was about time they saw something of the world.   We heard that Mr. Clark had a few moments' private conversation with Hiram in the

barn and Mr. Wheeler the same with his boys and
we do not think they will go traveling on their own
hook again right off. Miss Upham lives right
across the street from them and she was telling little
Morris Bates that he must fight the good fight of
faith and he asked her if that was the fight that
Wirt Wheeler fit. She probably had to make her
instructions plainer after that.

July.—Every Saturday our cousins, Lucilla and
Mary and Louisa Field, take turns coming to Grandmother's to dinner. It was Mary's turn to-day, but
she was sick and couldn't come, so Grandmother
told us that we could dress up and make some calls
for her. We were very glad. She told us to go
to Mrs. Gooding's first, so we did and she was glad
to see us and gave us some cake she had just made.
Then we went on to Mr. Greig's. We walked up
the high steps to the front door and rang the bell
and Mr. Alexander came. We asked if Mrs. Greig
and Miss Chapin were at home and he said yes, and
asked us into the parlor. We looked at the paintings on the wall and looked at ourselves in the long
looking-glass, while we were waiting. Mrs. Irving
came in first. She was very nice and said I looked
like her niece, Julie Jeffrey. I hope I do, for I
would like to look like her. Mrs. Greig and Miss
Chapin came in and were very glad to see us, and
took us out into the greenhouse and showed us all
the beautiful plants. When we said we would have

to go they said good-bye and sent love to Grandmother and told us to call again. I never knew
Anna to act as polite as she did to-day. Then we
went to see Mrs. Judge Phelps and Miss Eliza
Chapin, and they were very nice and gave us some
flowers from their garden. Then we went on to
Miss Caroline Jackson's, to see Mrs. Holmes.
Sometimes she is my Sunday School teacher, and
she says she and our mother used to be great friends
at the seminary. She said she was glad we came
up and she hoped we would be as good as our mother
was. That is what nearly every one says. On our
way back, we called on Mrs. Dana at the Academy,
as she is a friend of Grandmother. She is Mrs.
Noah T. Clarke's mother. After that, we went
home and told Grandmother we had a very pleasant
time calling on our friends and they all asked us to
come again.

Sunday, August 15.—To-day the Sacrament of
the Lord's Supper was held in our church, and Mr.
Daggett baptized several little babies. They looked
so cunning when he took them in his arms and not
one of them cried. I told Grandmother when we
got home that I remembered when Grandfather
Richards baptized me in Auburn, and when he gave
me back to mother he said, " Blessed little lambkin,
you'll never know your grandpa." She said I was
mistaken about remembering it, for he died before
I was a year old, but I had heard it told so many

times I thought I remembered it. Probably that
is the way it was but I know it happened.

November 22.—I wrote a composition to-day,
and the subject was, " Which of the Seasons Is the
Pleasantest? " Anna asked Grandmother what she
should write about, and Grandmother said she
thought " A Contented Mind " would be a very good
subject, but Anna said she never had one and didn't
know what it meant, so she didn't try to write any
at all.

A squaw walked right into our kitchen to-day with
a blanket over her head and had beaded purses to
sell.

This is my composition which I wrote : " Which
of the seasons is the pleasantest? Grim winter with
its cold snows and whistling winds, or pleasant
spring with its green grass and budding trees, or
warm summer with its ripening fruit and beautiful
flowers, or delightful autumn with its golden fruit
and splendid sunsets? I think that I like all the
seasons very well. In winter comes the blazing fire
and Christmas treat. Then we can have sleigh-
rides and play in the snow and generally get pretty
cold noses and toses. In spring we have a great
deal of rain and very often snow and therefore we
do not enjoy that season as much as we would if it
was dry weather, but we should remember that
April showers bring May flowers. In summer we
can hear the birds warbling their sweet notes in the

trees and we have a great many strawberries, cur-
rants, gooseberries and cherries, which I like very
much, indeed, and I think summer is a very pleasant
season. In autumn we have some of our choicest
fruits, such as peaches, pears, apples, grapes and
plums and plenty of flowers in the former part, but
in the latter, about in November, the wind begins
to blow and the leaves to fall and the flowers to
wither and die. Then cold winter with its sleigh-
rides comes round again." After I had written
this I went to bed. Anna tied her shoe strings in
hard knots so she could sit up later.

November 23.—We read our compositions to-day
and Miss Clark said mine was very good. One of
the girls had a Prophecy for a composition and told
what we were all going to be when we grew up.
She said Anna Richards was going to be a missionary and Anna cried right out loud. I tried to comfort her and told her it might never happen, so she
stopped crying.

November 24.—Three ladies visited our school
to-day, Miss Phelps, Miss Daniels and Mrs. Clark.
We had calisthenics and they liked them.

Sunday.—Mr. Tousley preached to-day. Mr.
Lamb is Superintendent of the Sunday School.
Mr. Chipman used to be. Miss Mollie Bull played
the melodeon. Mr. Fairchild is my teacher when he

is there. He was not there to-day and Miss Mary
Howell taught our class. I wish I could be as good
and pretty as she is. We go to church morning
and afternoon and to Sunday School, and learn
seven verses every week and recite catechism and
hymns to Grandmother in the evening. Grandmother knows all the questions by heart, so she lets
the book lie in her lap and she asks them with her
eyes shut. She likes to hear us sing:

> " 'Tis religion that can give
>   Sweetest pleasure while we live,
>   'Tis religion can supply
>   Solid comfort when we die."

December 1.—Grandfather asked me to read
President Pierce's message aloud to him this evening. I thought it was very long and dry, but he
said it was interesting and that I read it very well.
I am glad he liked it. Part of it was about the
Missouri Compromise and I didn't even know what
it meant.

December 8.—We are taking dictation lessons at
school now. Miss Clark reads to us from the " Life
of Queen Elizabeth " and we write it down in a
book and keep it. She corrects it for us. I always
spell " until " with two l's and she has to mark it
every time. I hope I will learn how to spell it
after a while.

Saturday, December 9.—We took our music lessons to-day. Miss Hattie Heard is our teacher and she says we are getting along well. Anna practiced her lesson over sixty-five times this morning before breakfast and can play " Mary to the Saviour's Tomb " as fast as a waltz.

We chose sides and spelled down at school to-day. Julia Phelps and I stood up the last and both went down on the same word—eulogism. I don't see the use of that " e." Miss Clark gave us twenty words which we had to bring into some stories which we wrote. It was real fun to hear them. Every one was different.

This evening as we sat before the fire place with Grandmother, she taught us how to play " Cat's Cradle," with a string on our fingers.

December 25.—Uncle Edward Richards sent us a basket of lovely things from New York for Christmas. Books and dresses for Anna and me, a kaleidoscope, large cornucopias of candy, and games, one of them being battledore and shuttlecock. Grandmother says we will have to wait until spring to play it, as it takes so much room. I wish all the little girls in the world had an Uncle Edward.

1854

January 1, 1854.—About fifty little boys and girls at intervals knocked at the front door to-day, to wish us Happy New Year. We had pennies and cakes and apples ready for them. The pennies, especially, seemed to attract them and we noticed the same ones several times. Aunt Mary Carr made lovely New Year cakes with a pretty flower stamped on before they were baked.

February 4, 1854.—We heard to-day of the death of our little half-sister, Julia Dey Richards, in Penn Yan, yesterday, and I felt so sorry I couldn't sleep last night so I made up some verses about her and this morning wrote them down and gave them to Grandfather. He liked them so well he wanted me to show them to Miss Clark and ask her to revise them. I did and she said she would hand them to her sister Mary to correct. When she handed them back they were very much nicer than they were at first and Grandfather had me copy them and he pasted them into one of his Bibles to keep.

Saturday.—Anna and I went to call on Miss Upham to-day. She is a real old lady and lives with her niece, Mrs. John Bates, on Gibson Street. Our mother used to go to school to her at the Seminary. Miss Upham said to Anna, " Your mother was a lovely woman. You are not at all like her, dear." I told Anna she meant in looks I was sure, but Anna was afraid she didn't.

Sunday.—Mr. Daggett's text this morning was the 22nd chapter of Revelation, 16th verse, " I am the root and offspring of David and the bright and morning star." Mrs. Judge Taylor taught our Sunday School class to-day and she said we ought not to read our S. S. books on Sunday. I always do. Mine to-day was entitled, " Cheap Repository Tracts by Hannah More," and it did not seem unreligious at all.

Tuesday.—A gentleman visited our school to-day whom we had never seen. Miss Clark introduced him to us. When he came in, Miss Clark said, " Young ladies," and we all stood up and bowed and said his name in concert. Grandfather says he would rather have us go to school to Miss Clark than any one else because she teaches us manners as well as books. We girls think that he is a very particular friend of Miss Clark. He is very nice looking, but we don't know where he lives. Laura Chapin says he is an architect. I looked it up in the dictionary and it says one who plans or designs. I hope he does not plan to get married to Miss Clark

and take her away and break up the school, but I
presume he does, for that is usually the way.

Monday.—There was a minister preached in our
church last night and some people say he is the
greatest minister in the world. I think his name
was Mr. Finney. Grandmother said I could go
with our girl, Hannah White. We sat under the
gallery, in Miss Antoinette Pierson's pew. There
was a great crowd and he preached good. Grandmother says that our mother was a Christian when
she was ten years old and joined the church and she
showed us some sermons that mother used to write
down when she was seventeen years old, after she
came home from church, and she has kept them all
these years. I think children in old times were not
as bad as they are now.

Tuesday.—Mrs. Judge Taylor sent for me to
come over to see her to-day. I didn't know what
she wanted, but when I got there she said she wanted
to talk and pray with me on the subject of religion.
She took me into one of the wings. I never had
been in there before and was frightened at first, but
it was nice after I got used to it. After she prayed,
she asked me to, but I couldn't think of anything
but "Now I lay me down to sleep," and I was afraid
she would not like that, so I didn't say anything.
When I got home and told Anna, she said, "Caroline, I presume probably Mrs. Taylor wants you to

be a Missionary, but I shan't let you go." I told her she needn't worry for I would have to stay at home and look after her. After school to-night I went out into Abbie Clark's garden with her and she taught me how to play " mumble te peg." It is fun, but rather dangerous. I am afraid Grandmother won't give me a knife to play with. Abbie Clark has beautiful pansies in her garden and gave me some roots.

April 1.—This is April Fool's Day. It is not a very pleasant day, but I am not very pleasant either. I spent half an hour this morning very pleasantly writing a letter to my Father but just as I had finished it, Grandmother told me something to write which I did not wish to and I spoke quite disrespectfully, but I am real sorry and I won't do so any more.

Lucilla and Louisa Field were over to our house to dinner to-day. We had a very good dinner indeed. In the afternoon, Grandmother told me that I might go over to Aunt Ann's on condition that I would not stay, but I stayed too long and got my indian rubbers real muddy and Grandmother did not like it. I then ate my supper and went to bed at ten minutes to eight o'clock.

Monday, April 3.—I got up this morning at quarter before six o'clock. I then read my three chapters in the Bible, and soon after ate my breakfast, which consisted of ham and eggs and buckwheat cakes. I then took a morning walk in the garden and rolled my hoop. I went to school at quarter before 9 o'clock. Miss Clark has us recite a verse of scripture in response to roll call and my text for the morning was the 8th verse of the 6th chapter of Matthew, " Be ye not therefore like unto them; for your Father knoweth what things ye have need of before ye ask him." We then had prayers. I then began to write my composition and we had recess soon after. In the afternoon I recited grammar, wrote my dictation lesson and Dictionary lesson. I was up third in my Dictionary class but missed two words, and instead of being third in the class, I was fifth. After supper I read my Sunday School book, " A Shepherd's Call to the Lambs of his Flock." I went to bed as usual at ten minutes to 8 o'clock.

April 4.—We went into our new schoolroom to-day at Miss Clark's school. It is a very nice room and much larger than the one we occupied before. Anna and I were sewing on our dolls' clothes this afternoon and we talked so much that finally Grandmother said, " the one that speaks first is the worst; and the one that speaks last is the best." We kept still for quite a while, which gave Grandmother a rest, but was very hard for us, especially Anna. Pretty soon Grandmother forgot and asked us a question, so we had the joke on her. Afterwards

Anna told me she would rather " be the worst," than
to keep still so long again.

Wednesday.—Grandmother sent Anna and me up
to Butcher Street after school to-day to invite Chloe
to come to dinner.   I never saw so many black people as there are up there.   We saw old Lloyd and
black Jonathan and Dick Valentine and Jerusha and
Chloe and Nackie.   Nackie was pounding up stones
into sand, to sell, to scour with.   Grandmother
often buys it of her.   I think Chloe was surprised,
but she said she would be ready, to-morrow, at
eleven o'clock, when the carriage came for her.   I
should hate to be as fat as Chloe.   I think she
weighs 300.   She is going to sit in Grandfather's
big arm chair, Grandmother says.

We told her we should think she would rather
invite white ladies, but she said Chloe was a poor
old slave and as Grandfather had gone to Saratoga
she thought it was a good time to have her.   She
said God made of one blood all the people on the
face of the earth, so we knew she would do it and
we didn't say any more.   When we talk too much,
Grandfather always says N. C. (nuff ced).   She
sent a carriage for Chloe and she came and had a
nice dinner, not in the kitchen either.   Grandmother
asked her if there was any one else she would like
to see before she went home and she said, " Yes,
Miss Rebekah Gorham," so she told the coachman
to take her down there and wait for her to make a

call and then take her home and he did. Chloe said she had a very nice time, so probably Grandmother was all right as she generally is, but I could not be as good as she is, if I should try one hundred years.

June.—Our cousin, George Bates, of Honolulu, came to see us to-day. He has one brother, Dudley, but he didn't come. George has just graduated from college and is going to Japan to be a doctor. He wrote such a nice piece in my album I must copy it, " If I were a poet I would celebrate your virtues in rhyme, if I were forty years old, I would write a homily on good behavior; being neither, I will quote two familiar lines which if taken as a rule of action will make you a good and happy woman :

" Honor and shame from no condition rise,
    Act well your part, there all the honor lies."

I think he is a very smart young man and will make a good doctor to the heathen.

Saturday.—Grandfather took us down street to be measured for some new patten leather shoes at Mr. Ambler's. They are going to be very nice ones for best. We got our new summer hats from Mrs. Freshour's millinery and we wore them over to

show to Aunt Ann and she said they were the very
handsomest bonnets she had seen this year.

Tuesday.—When we were on our way to school
this morning we met a lot of people and girls and
boys going to a picnic up the lake. They asked us
to go, too, but we said we were afraid we could not.
Mr. Alex. Howell said, " Tell your Grandfather I
will bring you back safe and sound unless the boat
goes to the bottom with all of us." So we went
home and told Grandfather and much to our surprise he said we could go. We had never been on
a boat or on the lake before. We went up to the
head on the steamer *" Joseph Wood "* and got off at
Maxwell's Point. They had a picnic dinner and
lots of good things to eat. Then we all went into
the glen and climbed up through it. Mr. Alex.
Howell and Mrs. Wheeler got to the top first and
everybody gave three cheers. We had a lovely time
riding back on the boat and told Grandmother we
had the very best time we ever had in our whole
lives.

May 26.—There was an eclipse of the sun to-day
and we were very much excited looking at it. General Granger came over and gave us some pieces of
smoked glass. Miss Clark wanted us to write compositions about it so Anna wrote, " About eleven
o'clock we went out to see if it had come yet, but
it hadn't come yet, so we waited awhile and then

looked again and it had come, and there was a piece
of it cut out of it." Miss Clark said it was a very
good description and she knew Anna wrote it all
herself.

I handed in a composition, too, about the eclipse,
but I don't think Miss Clark liked it as well as she
did Anna's, because it had something in it about
" the beggarly elements of the world." She asked
me where I got it and I told her that it was in a
nice story book that Grandmother gave me to read
entitled " Elizabeth Thornton or the Flower and
Fruit of Female Piety, and other sketches," by Samuel Irenaeus Prime. This was one of the other
sketches: It commenced by telling how the moon
came between the sun and the earth, and then went
on about the beggarly elements. Miss Clark
asked me if I knew what they meant and I told her
no, but I thought they sounded good. She just
smiled and never scolded me at all. I suppose next
time I must make it all up myself.

There is a Mr. Packer in town, who teaches all
the children to sing. He had a concert in Bemis
Hall last night and he put Anna on the top row of
the pyramid of beauty and about one hundred children in rows below. She ought to have worn a
white dress as the others did but Grandmother said
her new pink barege would do. I curled her hair
all around in about thirty curls and she looked very
nice. She waved the flag in the shape of the letter
S and sang " The Star Spangled Banner," and all

the others joined in the chorus. It was perfectly
grand.

Monday.—When we were on our way to school
this morning we saw General Granger coming, and
Anna had on such a homely sunbonnet she took it
off and hid it behind her till he had gone by. When
we told Grandmother she said, " Pride goeth before
destruction and a haughty spirit before a fall." I
never heard of any one who knew so many Bible
verses as Grandmother. Anna thought she would
be sorry for her and get her a new sunbonnet, but
she didn't.

Sunday.—We have Sunday School at nine o'clock
in the morning now. Grandfather loves to watch
us when we walk off together down the street, so
he walks back and forth on the front walk till we
come out, and gives us our money for the contribution. This morning we had on our new white
dresses that Miss Rosewarne made and new summer
hats and new patten leather shoes and our mitts.
When he had looked us all over he said, with a
smile, " The Bible says, let your garments be always
white." After we had gone on a little ways, Anna
said: " If Grandmother had thought of that verse
I wouldn't have had to wear my pink barege dress
to the concert." I told her she need not feel bad
about that now, for she sang as well as any of them
and looked just as good. She always believes every-

thing I say, although she does not always do what
I tell her to.   Mr. Noah T. Clarke told us in Sunday School last Sunday that if we wanted to take
shares in the missionary ship, *Morning Star,* we
could buy them at 10 cents apiece, and Grandmother
gave us $1 to-day so we could have ten shares.   We
got the certificate with a picture of the ship on it,
and we are going to keep it always.   Anna says if
we pay the money, we don't have to go.

Sunday.—I almost forgot that it was Sunday
this morning and talked and laughed just as I do
week days.   Grandmother told me to write down
this verse before I went to church so I would remember it: " Keep thy foot when thou goest to
the house of God, and be more ready to hear than
to offer the sacrifice of fools."   I will remember it
now, sure.   My feet are all right any way with my
new patten leather shoes on but I shall have to look
out for my head.   Mr. Thomas Howell read a sermon to-day as Mr. Daggett is out of town.   Grandmother always comes upstairs to get the candle and
tuck us in before she goes to bed herself, and some
nights we are sound asleep and do not hear her, but
last night we only pretended to be asleep.   She
kneeled down by the bed and prayed aloud for us,
that we might be good children and that she might
have strength given to her from on high to guide us
in the straight and narrow path which leads to life
eternal.   Those were her very words.   After she

Miss Upham

Mr. Noah T. Clarke

had gone downstairs we sat up in bed and talked
about it and promised each other to be good, and
crossed our hearts and " hoped to die " if we broke
our promise. Then Anna was afraid we would die,
but I told her I didn't believe we would be as
good as that, so we kissed each other and went to
sleep.

Monday.—" Old Alice " was at our house to-day
and Grandmother gave her some flowers. She hid
them in her apron for she said if she should meet
any little children and they should ask for them she
would have to let them go. Mrs. Gooding was at
our house to-day and made a carpet. We went
over to Aunt Mary Carr's this evening to see the
gas and the new chandeliers. They are brontz.

Tuesday.—My three chapters that I read this
morning were about Josiah's zeal and reformation;
2nd, Jerusalem taken by Nebuchadnezzar; 3rd, Jerusalem besieged and taken. The reason that we
always read the Bible the first thing in the morning is because it says in the Bible, " Seek first the
kingdom of God and His righteousness and all these
things shall be added unto you." Grandmother
says she hopes we will treasure up all these things
in our hearts and practice them in our lives. I hope
so, too. This morning Anna got very mad at one
of the girls and Grandmother told her she ought to

return good for evil and heap coals of fire on her head. Anna said she wished she could and burn her all up, but I don't think she meant it.

Wednesday.—I got up this morning at twenty minutes after five. I always brush my teeth every morning, but I forget to put it down here. I read my three chapters in Job and played in the garden and had time to read Grandmother a piece in the paper about some poor children in New York. Anna and I went over to Aunt Ann's before school and she gave us each two sticks of candy apiece. Part of it came from New York and part from Williamstown, Mass., where Henry goes to college. Ann Eliza is going down street with us this afternoon to buy us some new summer bonnets. They are to be trimmed with blue and white and are to come to five dollars. We are going to Mr. Stannard's store also, to buy us some stockings. I ought to buy me a new thimble and scissors for I carried my sewing to school to-day and they were inside of it very carelessly and dropped out and got lost. I ought to buy them with my own money, but I haven't got any, for I gave all I had (two shillings) to Anna to buy Louisa Field a cornelian ring. Perhaps Father will send me some money soon, but I hate to ask him for fear he will rob himself. I don't like to tell Grandfather how very careless I was, though I know he would say, " Accidents will happen."

Thursday.—I was up early this morning because a dressmaker, Miss Willson, is coming to make me a new calico dress. It is white with pink spots in it and Grandfather bought it in New York. It is very nice indeed and I think Grandfather was very kind to get it for me. I had to stay at home from school to be fitted. I helped sew and run my dress skirt around the bottom and whipped it on the top. I went to school in the afternoon, but did not have my lessons very well. Miss Clark excused me because I was not there in the morning. Some girls got up on our fence to-day and walked clear across it, the whole length. It is iron and very high and has a stone foundation. Grandmother asked them to get down, but I think they thought it was more fun to walk up there than it was on the ground. The name of the little girl that got up first was Mary Lapham. She is Lottie Lapham's cousin. I made the pocket for my dress after I got home from school and then Grandfather said he would take us out to ride, so he took us way up to Thaddeus Chapin's on the hill. Julia Phelps was there, playing with Laura Chapin, for she is her cousin. Henry and Ann Eliza Field came over to call this evening. Henry has come home from Williams College on his vacation and he is a very pleasant young man, indeed. I am reading a continued story in *Harper's Magazine*. It is called Little Dorritt, by Charles Dickens, and is very interesting.

Friday, May.—Miss Clark told us we could have
a picnic down to Sucker Brook this afternoon and
she told us to bring our rubbers and lunches by two
o'clock; but Grandmother was not willing to let us
go; not that she wished to deprive us of any pleasure
for she said instead we could wear our new black
silk basks and go with her to Preparatory lecture,
so we did, but when we got there we found that
Mr. Daggett was out of town so there was no meeting.   Then she told us we could keep dressed up and
go over to Aunt Mary Carr's and take her some
apples, and afterwards Grandfather took us to ride
to see old Mrs. Sanborn and old Mr. and Mrs. Atwater.   He is ninety years old and blind and deaf,
so we had quite a good time after all.

Rev. Mr. Dickey, of Rochester, agent for the
Seaman's Friend Society, preached this morning
about the poor little canal boy.   His text was from
the 107th Psalm, 23rd verse, " They that go down
into the sea in ships."   He has the queerest voice
and stops off between his words.   When we got
home Anna said she would show us how he preached
and she described what he said about a sailor in
time of war.   She said, " A ball came—and struck
him there—another ball came—and struck him
there—he raised his faithful sword—and went on—
to victory—or death."   I expected Grandfather
would reprove her, but he just smiled a queer sort
of smile and Grandmother put her handkerchief up
to her face, as she always does when she is amused

about anything. I never heard her laugh out loud, but I suppose she likes funny things as well as anybody. She did just the same, this morning, when Grandfather asked Anna where the sun rose, and she said "over by Gen. Granger's house and sets behind the Methodist church." She said she saw it herself and should never forget it when any one asked her which was east or west. I think she makes up more things than any one I know of.

Sunday.—Rev. M. L. R. P. Thompson preached to-day. He used to be the minister of our church before Mr. Daggett came. Some people call him Rev. "Alphabet" Thompson, because he has so many letters in his name. He preached a very good sermon from the text, "Dearly beloved, as much as lieth in you, live peaceably with all men." I like to hear him preach, but not as well as I do Mr. Daggett. I suppose I am more used to him.

Thursday.—Edward Everett, of Boston, lectured in our church this evening. They had a platform built even with the tops of the pews, so he did not have to go up into the pulpit. Crowds and crowds came to hear him from all over everywhere. Grandmother let me go. They say he is the most eloquent speaker in the U. S., but I have heard Mr. Daggett when I thought he was just as good.

Sunday.—We went to church to-day and heard
Rev. Mr. Stowe preach. His text was, " The poor
ye have with you always and whensoever ye will ye
may do them good." I never knew any one who
liked to go to church as much as Grandmother does.
She says she " would rather be a doorkeeper in the
house of our God, than to dwell in the tents of wick-
edness." They don't have women doorkeepers, and
I know she would not dwell a minute in a tent. Mr.
Coburn is the doorkeeper in our church and he rings
the bell every day at nine in the morning and at
twelve and at nine in the evening, so Grandfather
knows when it is time to cover up the fire in the
fireplace and go to bed. I think if the President
should come to call he would have to go home at
nine o'clock. Grandfather's motto is:

> " Early to bed and early to rise
> Makes a man healthy, wealthy and wise."

Tuesday.—Mrs. Greig and Miss Chapin called to
see us to-day. Grandmother says that we can return the calls as she does not visit any more. We
would like to, for we always enjoy dressing up and
making calls. Anna and I received two black veils
in a letter to-day from Aunt Caroline Dey. Just
exactly what we had wanted for a long while.
Uncle Edward sent us five dollars and Grandmother
said we could buy just what we wanted, so we went
down street to look at black silk mantillas. We

went to Moore's store and to Richardson's and to Collier's, but they asked ten, fifteen or twenty dollars for them, so Anna said she resolved from now, henceforth and forever not to spend her money for black silk mantillas.

Sunday.—Rev. Mr. Tousley preached to-day to the children and told us how many steps it took to be bad. I think he said lying was first, then disobedience to parents, breaking the Sabbath, swearing, stealing, drunkenness. I don't remember just the order they came. It was very interesting, for he told lots of stories and we sang a great many times. I should think Eddy Tousley would be an awful good boy with his father in the house with him all the while, but probably he has to be away part of the time preaching to other children.

Sunday.—Uncle David Dudley Field and his daughter, Mrs. Brewer, of Stockbridge, Mass., are visiting us. Mrs. Brewer has a son, David Josiah, who is in Yale College. After he graduates he is going to be a lawyer and study in his Uncle David Dudley Field's office in New York. He was born in Smyrna, Asia Minor, where his father and mother were missionaries to the Greeks, in 1837. Our Uncle David preached for Mr. Daggett this afternoon. He is a very old man and left his sermon at home and I had to go back after it. His brother, Timothy, was the first minister in our

church, about fifty years ago. Grandmother says
she came all the way from Connecticut with him
on horseback on a pillion behind him. Rather a
long ride, I should say. I heard her and Uncle
David talking about their childhood and how they
lived in Guilford, Conn., in a house that was built
upon a rock. That was some time in the last century like the house that it tells about in the Bible
that was built on a rock.

Sunday, August 10, 1854.—Rev. Mr. Daggett's
text this morning was, " Remember the Sabbath
day to keep it holy." Grandmother said she
thought the sermon did not do us much good for
she had to tell us several times this afternoon to
stop laughing. Grandmother said we ought to be
good Sundays if we want to go to heaven, for there
it is one eternal Sabbath. Anna said she didn't
want to be an angel just yet and I don't think there
is the least danger of it, as far as I can judge.
Grandmother said there was another verse, " If we
do not have any pleasure on the Sabbath, or think
any thoughts, we shall ride on the high places of
the earth," and Anna said she liked that better, for
she would rather ride than do anything else, so we
both promised to be good. Grandfather told us
they used to be more strict about Sunday than they
are now. Then he told us a story, how he had to
go to Geneva one Saturday morning in the stage
and expected to come back in the evening, but there

First Congregational Church

was an accident, so the stage did not come till Sunday morning. Church had begun and he told the stage driver to leave him right there, so he went in late and the stage drove on. The next day he heard that he was to come before the minister, Rev. Mr. Johns, and the deacons and explain wny he had broken the fourth commandment. When he got into the meeting Mr. Johns asked him what he had to say, and he explained about the accident and asked them to read a verse from the 8th chapter of John, before they made up their minds what to do to him. The verse was, "Let him that is without sin among you cast the first stone." Grandfather said they all smiled, and the minister said the meeting was out. Grandfather says that shows it is better to know plenty of Bible verses, for some time they may do you a great deal of good. We then recited the catechism and went to bed.

August 21.—Anna says that Alice Jewett feels very proud because she has a little baby brother. They have named him John Harvey Jewett after his father, and Alice says when he is bigger she will let Anna help her take him out to ride in his baby-carriage. I suppose they will throw away their dolls now.

Tuesday, September 1.—I am sewing a sheet over and over for Grandmother and she puts a pin in to show me my stint, before I can go out to play.

I am always glad when I get to it. I am making a sampler, too, and have all the capital letters worked and now will make the small ones. It is done in cross stitch on canvas with different color silks. I am going to work my name, too. I am also knitting a tippet on some wooden needles that Henry Carr made for me. Grandmother has raveled it out several times because I dropped stitches. It is rather tedious, but she says, " If at first you don't succeed, try, try again." Some military soldiers went by the house to-day and played some beautiful music. Grandfather has a teter and swing for us in the back yard and we enjoy them usually, but to-night Anna slid off the teter board when she was on the ground and I was in the air and I came down sooner than I expected. There was a hand organ and monkey going by and she was in a hurry to get to the street to see it. She got there a good while before I did. The other day we were swinging and Grandmother called us in to dinner, but Anna said we could not go until we " let the old cat die." Grandmother said it was more important that we should come when we are called.

October.—Grandmother's name is Abigail, but she was always called " Nabby " at home. Some of the girls call me " Carrie," but Grandmother prefers " Caroline." She told us to-day, how when she was a little girl, down in Connecticut in 1794, she was on her way to school one morning and she saw

an Indian coming and was so afraid, but did not
dare run for fear he would chase her. So she
thought of the word sago, which means "good
morning," and when she got up close to him she
dropped a curtesy and said "Sago," and he just
went right along and never touched her at all. She
says she hopes we will always be polite to every
one, even to strangers.

November.—Abbie Clark's father has been elected
Governor and she is going to Albany to live, for a
while. We all congratulated her when she came to
school this morning, but I am sorry she is going
away. We will write to each other every week.
She wrote a prophecy and told the girls what they
were going to be and said I should be mistress of
the White House. I think it will happen, about the
same time that Anna goes to be a missionary.

December.—There was a moonlight sleighride of
boys and girls last night, but Grandfather did not
want us to go, but to-night he said he was going to
take us to one himself. So after supper he told
Mr. Piser to harness the horse to the cutter and
bring it around to the front gate. Mr. Piser takes
care of our horse and the Methodist Church. He
lives in the basement. Grandfather sometimes calls
him Shakespeare to us, but I don't know why. He
doesn't look as though he wrote poetry. Grandfather said he was going to take us out to Mr.

Waterman Powers' in Farmington and he did. They were quite surprised to see us, but very glad and gave us apples and doughnuts and other good things. We saw Anne and Imogene and Morey and one little girl named Zimmie. They wanted us to stay all night, but Grandmother was expecting us. We got home safe about ten o'clock and had a very nice time. We never sat up so late before.

1855

Wednesday, January 9.—I came downstairs this morning at ten minutes after seven, almost frozen. I never spent such a cold night before in all my life. It is almost impossible to get warm even in the dining-room. The thermometer is 10° below zero. The schoolroom was so cold that I had to keep my cloak on. I spoke a piece this afternoon. It was " The Old Arm Chair," by Eliza Cook. It begins, " I love it, I love it, and who shall dare to chide me for loving that old arm chair? " I love it because it makes me think of Grandmother. After school to-night Anna and I went downtown to buy a writing book, but we were so cold we thought we would never get back. Anna said she knew her toes were frozen. We got as far as Mr. Taylor's gate and she said she could not get any farther; but I pulled her along, for I could not bear to have her perish in sight of home. We went to bed about eight o'clock and slept very nicely indeed, for Grandmother put a good many blankets on and we were warm.

January 23.—This evening after reading one of Dickens' stories I knit awhile on my mittens. I

have not had nice ones in a good while. Grandmother cut out the ones that I am wearing of white
flannel, bound round the wrist with blue merino.
They are not beautiful to be sure, but warm and
will answer all purposes until I get some that are
better. When I came home from school to-day
Mrs. Taylor was here. She noticed how tall I was
growing and said she hoped that I was as good as
I was tall. A very good wish, I am sure.

Sunday, January 29.—Mr. Daggett preached this
morning from the text, Deut. 8: 2: "And thou
shalt remember all the way which the Lord thy God
led thee." It is ten years to-day since Mr. Daggett
came to our church, and he told how many deaths
there had been, and how many baptisms, and how
many members had been added to the church. It
was a very interesting sermon, and everybody hoped
Mr. Daggett would stay here ten years more, or
twenty, or thirty, or always. He is the only minister that I ever had, and I don't ever want any other.
We never could have any one with such a voice as
Mr. Daggett's, or such beautiful eyes. Then he has
such good sermons, and always selects the hymns
we like best, and reads them in such a way. This
morning they sang: "Thus far the Lord has led
me on, thus far His power prolongs my days."
After he has been away on a vacation he always
has for the first hymn, and we always turn to it
before he gives it out:

> "Upward I lift mine eyes,
> From God is all my aid;
> The God that built the skies,
> And earth and nature made.
>
> "God is the tower
> To which I fly
> His grace is nigh
> In every hour."

He always prays for the oil of joy for mourning and the garment of praise for the spirit of heaviness.

January, 1855.—Johnny Lyon is dead. Georgia Wilkinson cried awfully in school because she said she was engaged to him.

April.—Grandmother received a letter from Connecticut to-day telling of the death of her only sister. She was knitting before she got it and she laid it down a few moments and looked quite sad and said, "So sister Anna is dead." Then after a little she went on with her work. Anna watched her and when we were alone she said to me, "Caroline, some day when you are about ninety you may be eating an apple or reading or doing something and you will get a letter telling of my decease and after you have read it you will go on as usual and just say, 'So sister Anna is dead.'" I told her that I knew if I lived to be a hundred and heard that she was dead I should cry my eyes out, if I had any.

May.—Father has sent us a box of fruit from New Orleans. Prunes, figs, dates and oranges, and one or two pomegranates. We never saw any of the latter before. They are full of cells with jelly in, very nice. He also sent some seeds of sensitive plant, which we have sown in our garden.

This evening I wrote a letter to John and a little " poetry " to Father, but it did not amount to much. I am going to write some a great deal better some day. Grandfather had some letters to write this morning, and got up before three o'clock to write them! He slept about three-quarters of an hour to-night in his chair.

Sunday.—There was a stranger preached for Dr. Daggett this morning and his text was, " Man looketh upon the outward appearance but the Lord looketh on the heart." When we got home Anna said the minister looked as though he had been sick from birth and his forehead stretched from his nose to the back of his neck, he was so bald. Grandmother told her she ought to have been more interested in his words than in his looks, and that she must have very good eyes if she could see all that from our pew, which is the furthest from the pulpit of any in church, except Mr. Gibson's, which is just the same. Anna said she couldn't help seeing it unless she shut her eyes, and then every one would think she had gone to sleep. We can see the Academy boys from our pew, too.

Mr. Lathrop, of the seminary, is superintendent of the Sunday School now and he had a present to-day from Miss Betsey Chapin, and several visitors came in to see it presented: Dr. Daggett, Mr. and Mrs. Alex. Howell, Mr. Tousley, Mr. Stowe, Mr. and Mrs. Gideon Granger and several others. The present was a certificate of life membership to something; I did not hear what. It was just a large piece of parchment, but they said it cost $25. Miss Lizzie Bull is my Sunday School teacher now. She asked us last Sunday to look up a place in the Bible where the trees held a consultation together, to see which one should reign over them. I did not remember any such thing, but I looked it up in the concordance and found it in Judges 9: 8. I found the meaning of it in Scott's Commentary and wrote it down and she was very much pleased, and told us next Sunday to find out all about Absalom.

July.—Our sensitive plant is growing nicely and it is quite a curiosity. It has fern-like leaves and when we touch them, they close, but soon come out again. Anna and I keep them performing.

September 1.—Anna and I go to the seminary now. Mr. Richards and Mr. Tyler are the principals. Anna fell down and sprained her ankle to-day at the seminary, and had to be carried into Mrs. Richards' library. She was sliding down the bannisters with little Annie Richards. I wonder what she will do next. She has good luck in the gym-

nasium and can beat Emma Wheeler and Jennie
Ruckle swinging on the pole and climbing the rope
ladder, although they and Sarah Antes are about as
spry as squirrels and they are all good at ten pins.
Susie Daggett and Lucilla Field have gone to Farmington, Conn., to school.

Monday.—I received a letter from my brother
John in New Orleans, and his ambrotype. He has
grown amazingly. He also sent me a N. O. paper
and it gave an account of the public exercises in the
school, and said John spoke a piece called " The
Baron's Last Banquet," and had great applause and
it said he was " a chip off the old block." He is a
very nice boy, I know that. James is sixteen years
old now and is in Princeton College. He is studying
German and says he thinks he will go to Germany
some day and finish his education, but I guess in
that respect he will be very much disappointed.
Germany is a great ways off and none of our rela-
tions that I ever heard of have ever been there and
it is not at all likely that any of them ever will.
Grandfather says, though, it is better to aim too high
than not high enough. James is a great boy to
study. They had their pictures taken together once
and John was holding some flowers and James a
book and I guess he has held on to it ever since.

Sunday.—Polly Peck looked so funny on the
front seat of the gallery. She had on one of Mrs.

Greig's bonnets and her lace collar and cape and mitts. She used to be a milliner so she knows how to get herself up in style. The ministers have appointed a day of fasting and prayer and Anna asked Grandmother if it meant to eat as fast as you can. Grandmother was very much surprised.

November 25.—I helped Grandmother get ready for Thanksgiving Day by stoning some raisins and pounding some cloves and cinnamon in the mortar pestle pounder. It is quite a job. I have been writing with a quill pen but I don't like it because it squeaks so. Grandfather made us some to-day and also bought us some wafers to seal our letters with, and some sealing wax and a stamp with " R " on it. He always uses the seal on his watch fob with " B." He got some sand, too. Our inkstand is double and has one bottle for ink and the other for sand to dry the writing.

December 20, 1855.—Susan B. Anthony is in town and spoke in Bemis Hall this afternoon. She made a special request that all the seminary girls should come to hear her as well as all the women and girls in town. She had a large audience and she talked very plainly about our rights and how we ought to stand up for them, and said the world would never go right until the women had just as much right to vote and rule as the men. She asked us all to come up and sign our names who would promise to do all in our power to bring about that glad day when equal rights should be the law of the land. A whole lot of us went up and signed the paper. When I told Grandmother about it she said she guessed Susan B. Anthony had forgotten that St. Paul said the women should keep silence. I told her, no, she didn't for she spoke particularly about St. Paul and said if he had lived in these times, instead of 1800 years ago, he would have been as anxious to have the women at the head of the government as she was. I could not make Grandmother agree with her at all and she said we might better all of us stayed at home. We went to prayer meeting this evening and a woman got up and talked. Her name was Mrs. Sands. We hurried home and told Grandmother and she said she probably meant all right and she hoped we did not laugh.

Monday.—I told Grandfather if he would bring me some sheets of foolscap paper I would begin to write a book. So he put a pin on his sleeve to remind him of it and to-night he brought me a whole lot of it. I shall begin it to-morrow. This evening I helped Anna do her Arithmetic examples, and read her Sunday School book. The name of it is " Watch and Pray." My book is the second volume of " Stories on the Shorter Catechism."

Tuesday.—I decided to copy a lot of choice stories and have them printed and say they were " compiled

by Caroline Cowles Richards," it is so much easier
than making them up. I spent three hours to-day
copying one and am so tired I think I shall give it up.
When I told Grandmother she looked disappointed
and said my ambition was like " the morning cloud
and the early dew," for it soon vanished away. Anna
said it might spring up again and bear fruit a hun-
dredfold. Grandfather wants us to amount to
something and he buys us good books whenever he
has a chance. He bought me Miss Caroline Chesebro's book, " The Children of Light," and Alice and
Phoebe Cary's *Poems*. He is always reading Channing's memoirs and sermons and Grandmother
keeps " Lady Huntington and Her Friends," next to
" Jay's Morning and Evening Exercises " and her
Testament. Anna told Grandmother that she saw
Mrs. George Willson looking very steadily at us in
prayer meeting the other night and she thought
she might be planning to " write us up." Grandmother said she did not think Mrs. Willson was so
short of material as that would imply, and she
feared she had some other reason for looking at us.
I think dear Grandmother has a little grain of sar-
casm in her nature, but she only uses it on extra
occasions. Anna said, " Oh, no; she wrote the lives
of the three Mrs. Judsons and I thought she might
like for a change to write the biographies of the
' two Miss Richards.' " Anna has what might be
called a vivid imagination.

1856

January 23.—This is the third morning that I have come down stairs at exactly twenty minutes to seven. I went to school all day. Mary Paul and Fannie Palmer read *"The Snow Bird"* to-day. There were some funny things in it. One was: "Why is a lady's hair like the latest news? Because in the morning we always find it in the papers." Another was: "One rod makes an acher, as the boy said when the schoolmaster flogged him."

This is Allie Field's birthday. He got a pair of slippers from Mary with the soles all on; a pair of mittens from Miss Eliza Chapin, and Miss Rebecca Gorham is going to give him a pair of stockings when she gets them done.

January 30.—I came home from school at eleven o'clock this morning and learned a piece to speak this afternoon, but when I got up to school I forgot it, so I thought of another one. Mr. Richards said that he must give me the praise of being the best speaker that spoke in the afternoon. Ahem!

February 6.—We were awakened very early this morning by the cry of fire and the ringing of bells and could see the sky red with flames and knew it was the stores and we thought they were all burning up. Pretty soon we heard our big brass door knocker being pounded fast and Grandfather said, " Who's there? " " Melville Arnold for the bank keys," we heard. Grandfather handed them out and dressed as fast as he could and went down, while Anna and I just lay there and watched the flames and shook. He was gone two or three hours and when he came back he said that Mr. Palmer's hat store, Mr. Underhill's book store, Mr. Shafer's tailor shop, Mrs. Smith's millinery, Pratt & Smith's drug store, Mr. Mitchell's dry goods store, two printing offices and a saloon were burned. It was a very handsome block. The bank escaped fire, but the wall of the next building fell on it and crushed it. After school to-night Grandmother let us go down to see how the fire looked. It looked very sad indeed. Judge Taylor offered Grandfather one of the wings of his house for the bank for the present but he has secured a place in Mr. Buhre's store in the Franklin Block.

Thursday, February 7.—Dr. and Aunt Mary Carr and Uncle Field and Aunt Ann were over at our house to dinner to-day and we had a fine fish dinner, not one of Gabriel's (the man who blows such a blast through the street, they call him Gabriel), but one that Mr. Francis Granger sent to us. It was elegant. Such a large one it covered a big platter. This evening General Granger came in and brought

a gentleman with him whose name was Mr. Skinner.
They asked Grandfather, as one of the trustees of
the church, if he had any objection to a deaf and
dumb exhibition there to-morrow night. He had
no objection, so they will have it and we will go.

Friday.—We went and liked it very much. The
man with them could talk and he interpreted it.
There were two deaf and dumb women and three
children. They performed very prettily, but the
smartest boy did the most. He acted out David killing Goliath and the story of the boy stealing apples
and how the old man tried to get him down by
throwing grass at him, but finding that would not
do, he threw stones which brought the boy down
pretty quick. Then he acted a boy going fishing
and a man being shaved in a barber shop and several
other things. I laughed out loud in school to-day
and made some pictures on my slate and showed
them to Clara Willson and made her laugh, and
then we both had to stay after school. Anna was at
Aunt Ann's to supper to-night to meet a little girl
named Helen Bristol, of Rochester. Ritie Tyler
was there, too, and they had a lovely time.

February 8.—I have not written in my journal
for several days, because I never like to write things
down if they don't go right. Anna and I were
invited to go on a sleigh-ride, Tuesday night, and
Grandfather said he did not want us to go. We

Judge Henry W. Taylor   Miss Zilpha Clark

Rev. Oliver E. Daggett, D.D.

"Frankie Richardson"   Horace Finley

asked him if we could spend the evening with
Frankie Richardson and he said yes, so we went
down there and when the load stopped for her, we
went too, but we did not enjoy ourselves at all and
did not join in the singing. I had no idea that
sleigh-rides could make any one feel so bad. It was
not very cold, but I just shivered all the time.
When the nine o'clock bell rang we were up by the
" Northern Retreat," and I was so glad when we got
near home so we could get out. Grandfather and
Grandmother asked us if we had a nice time, but
we got to bed as quick as we could. The next day
Grandfather went into Mr. Richardson's store and
told him he was glad he did not let Frankie go on
the sleigh-ride, and Mr. Richardson said he did let
her go and we went too. We knew how it was
when we got home from school, because they acted
so sober, and, after a while, Grandmother talked
with us about it. We told her we were sorry and
we did not have a bit good time and would never
do it again. When she prayed with us the next
morning, as she always does before we go to school,
she said, " Prepare us, Lord, for what thou art preparing for us," and it seemed as though she was
discouraged, but she said she forgave us. I know
one thing, we will never run away to any more
sleigh-rides.

February 20.—Mr. Worden, Mrs. Henry Chesebro's father, was buried to-day, and Aunt Ann let

Allie stay with us while she went to the funeral. I am going to Fannie Gaylord's party to-morrow night.

I went to school this afternoon and kept the rules, so to-night I had the satisfaction of saying " perfect " when called upon, and if I did not like to keep the rules, it is some pleasure to say that.

February 21.—We had a very nice time at Fannie Gaylord's party and a splendid supper. Lucilla Field laughed herself almost to pieces when she found on going home that she had worn her leggins all the evening. We had a pleasant walk home but did not stay till it was out. Some one asked me if I danced every set and I told them no, I set every dance. I told Grandmother and she was very much pleased. Some one told us that Grandfather and Grandmother first met at a ball in the early settlement of Canandaigua. I asked her if it was so and she said she never had danced since she became a professing Christian and that was more than fifty years ago.

Grandfather heard to-day of the death of his sister, Lydia, who was Mrs. Lyman Beecher. She was Rev. Dr. Lyman Beecher's third wife. Grandmother says that they visited her once and she was quite nervous thinking about having such a great man as Dr. Lyman Beecher for her guest, as he was considered one of the greatest men of his day, but she said she soon got over this feeling, for he was

so genial and pleasant and she noticed particularly
how he ran up and down stairs like a boy.   I think
that is very apt to be the way for " men are only
boys grown tall."

There was a Know Nothing convention in town
to-day.   They don't want any one but Americans to
hold office, but I guess they will find that foreigners
will get in.   Our hired man is an Irishman and I
think he would just as soon be " Prisidint " as not.

February 22.—This is such a beautiful day, the
girls wanted a holiday, but Mr. Richards would not
grant it.   We told him it was Washington's birthday and we felt very patriotic, but he was inexo-
rable.   We had a musical review and literary exercises instead in the afternoon and I put on my blue
merino dress and my other shoes.   Anna dressed
up, too, and I curled her hair.   The Primary scholars sit upstairs this term and do not have to pay
any more.   Anna and Emma Wheeler like it very
much, but they do not sit together.   We are seated
alphabetically, and I sit with Mary Reznor and Anna
with Mittie Smith.   They thought she would behave
better, I suppose, if they put her with one of the
older girls, but I do not know as it will have the
" desired effect," as Grandmother says.   Miss Mary
Howell and Miss Carrie Hart and Miss Lizzie and
Miss Mollie Bull were visitors this afternoon.   Ger-
trude Monier played and sang.   Mrs. Anderson is
the singing teacher.   Marion Maddox and Pussie

Harris and Mary Daniels played on the piano.   Mr.
Hardick is the teacher, and he played too.   You
would think he was trying to pound the piano all
to pieces but he is a good player.   We have two
papers kept up at school, *The Snow Bird* and *The
Waif*—one for the younger and the other for the
older girls.   Miss Jones, the composition teacher,
corrects them both.   Kate Buell and Anna Maria
Chapin read *The Waif* to-day and Gusta Buell and
I read *The Snow Bird*.   She has beautiful curls and
has two nice brothers also, Albert and Arthur, and
the girls all like them.   They have not lived in town
very long.

February 25.—I guess I won't fill up my journal
any more by saying I arose this morning at the usual
time, for I don't think it is a matter of life or death
whether I get up at the usual time or a few minutes
later and when I am older and read over the account
of the manner in which I occupied my time in my
younger days I don't think it will add particularly
to the interest to know whether I used to get up
at 7 or at a quarter before.   I think Miss Sprague,
our schoolroom teacher, would have been glad if
none of us had got up at all this morning for we
acted so in school.   She does not want any noise
during the three minute recess, but there has been a
good deal all day.   In singing class they disturbed
Mr. Kimball by blowing through combs.   We took
off our round combs and put paper over them and

then blew—Mary Wheeler and Lottie Lapham and Anna sat nearest me and we all tried to do it, but Lottie was the only one who could make it go. He thought we all did, so he made us come up and sit by him. I did not want to a bit. He told Miss Sprague of us and she told the whole school if there was as much noise another day she would keep every one of us an hour after half-past 4. As soon as she said this they all began to groan. She said " Silence." I only made the least speck of a noise that no one heard.

February 26.—To-night, after singing class, Mr. Richards asked all who blew through combs to rise. I did not, because I could not make it go, but when he said all who groaned could rise, I did, and some others, but not half who did it. He kept us very late and we all had to sign an apology to Miss Sprague.

Grandfather made me a present of a beautiful blue stone to-day called Malachite. Anna said she always thought Malachite was one of the prophets.

March 3, 1856.—Elizabeth Spencer sits with me in school now. She is full of fun but always manages to look very sober when Miss Chesebro looks up to see who is making the noise over our way. I never seem to have that knack. Anna had to stay after school last night and she wrote in her journal that the reason was because " nature will out " and because " she whispered and didn't have her lessons, etc., etc., etc." Mr. Richards has allowed us to bring our sewing to school but now he says we cannot any more. I am sorry for I have some embroidery and I could get one pantalette done in a week, but now it will take me longer. Grandmother has offered me one dollar if I will stitch a linen shirt bosom and wrist bands for Grandfather and make the sleeves. I have commenced but, Oh my! it is an undertaking. I have to pull the threads out and then take up two threads and leave three. It is very particular work and Anna says the stitches must not be visible to the naked eye. I have to fell the sleeves with the tiniest seams and stroke all the gathers and put a stitch on each gather. Minnie Bellows is the best one in school with her needle and is a dabster at patching. She cut a piece right out of her new calico dress and matched a new piece in and none of us could tell where it was. I am sure it would not be safe for me to try that. Grandmother let me ask three of the girls to dinner Saturday, Abbie Clark, Mary Wheeler and Mary Field. We had a big roast turkey and everything else to match. Good enough for Queen Victoria. That reminds me of a conundrum we had in *The Snow Bird:* What does Queen Victoria take her pills in? In cider. (Inside her.)

March 7.—The reports were read at school to-day and mine was, Attendance 10, Deportment 8, Scholarship 7½, and Anna's 10, 10 and 7. I think they got it turned around, for Anna has not behaved anything uncommon lately.

March 10.—My teacher Miss Sprague kept me after school to-night for whispering, and after all the others were gone she came to my seat and put her arm around me and kissed me and said she loved me very much and hoped I would not whisper in school any more. This made me feel very sorry and I told her I would try my best, but it seemed as though it whispered itself sometimes. I think she is just as nice as she can be and I shall tell the other girls so. Her home is in Glens Falls.

Anna jumped the rope two hundred times to-day without stopping, and I told her that I read of a girl who did that and then fell right down stone dead. I don't believe Anna will do it again. If she does I shall tell Grandmother.

April 5.—I walked down town with Grandfather this morning and it is such a beautiful day I felt glad that I was alive. The air was full of tiny little flies, buzzing around and going in circles and semicircles as though they were practising calisthenics or dancing a quadrille. I think they were glad they were alive, too. I stepped on a big bug crawling on the walk and Grandfather said I ought to have brushed it aside instead of killing it. I asked him why and he said, " Shakespeare says, ' The beetle that we tread upon feels a pang as great as when a giant dies.' "

A man came to our door the other day and asked if " Deacon " Beals was at home. I asked Grandmother afterwards if Grandfather was a Deacon and she said no and never had been, that people gave him the name when he was a young man because he was so staid and sober in his appearance. Some one told me once that I would not know my Grandfather if I should meet him outside the Corporation. I asked why and he said because he was so genial and told such good stories. I told him that was just the way he always is at home. I do not know any one who appreciates real wit more than he does. He is quite strong in his likes and dislikes, however. I have heard him say,

> " I do not like you, Dr. Fell,
> The reason why, I cannot tell ;
> But this one thing I know full well,
> I do not like you, Dr. Fell."

Bessie Seymour wore a beautiful gold chain to school this morning and I told Grandmother that I wanted one just like it. She said that outward adornments were not of as much value as inward graces and the ornament of a meek and quiet spirit, in the sight of the Lord, was of great price. I know it is very becoming to Grandmother and she wears it all the time but I wish I had a gold chain just the same.

Aunt Ann received a letter to-day from Lucilla, who is at Miss Porter's school at Farmington, Connecticut. She feels as if she were a Christian and that she has experienced religion.

Grandfather noticed how bright and smart Bentley Murray was, on the street, and what a business way he had, so he applied for a place for him as page in the Legislature at Albany and got it. He is always noticing young people and says, " As the twig is bent, the tree is inclined." He says we may be teachers yet if we are studious now. Anna says, " Excuse me, please."

Grandmother knows the Bible from Genesis to Revelation excepting the " begats " and the hard names, but Anna told her a new verse this morning, " At Parbar westward, four at the causeway and two at Parbar." Grandmother put her spectacles up on her forehead and just looked at Anna as though she had been talking in Chinese. She finally said, " Anna, I do not think that is in the Bible." She said, " Yes, it is; I found it in 1 Chron. 26: 18." Grandmother found it and then she said Anna had better spend her time looking up more helpful texts. Anna then asked her if she knew who was the shortest man mentioned in the Bible and Grandmother said " Zaccheus." Anna said that she just read in the newspaper, that one said " Nehimiah was " and another said " Bildad the Shuhite " and another said " Tohi." Grandmother said it was very wicked to pervert the Scripture so, and she did not approve of

it at all.   I don't think Anna will give Grandmother
any more Bible conundrums.

April 12.—We went down town this morning and
bought us some shaker bonnets to wear to school.
They cost $1 apiece and we got some green silk for
capes to put on them.   We fixed them ourselves
and wore them to school and some of the girls liked
them and some did not, but it makes no difference
to me what they like, for I shall wear mine till it
is worn out.   Grandmother says that if we try to
please everybody we please nobody.   The girls are
all having mystic books at school now and they are
very interesting to have.   They are blank books and
we ask the girls and boys to write in them and then
they fold the page twice over and seal it with wafers
or wax and then write on it what day it is to be
opened.   Some of them say, " Not to be opened for
a year," and that is a long time to wait.   If we cannot wait we can open them and seal them up again.
I think Anna did look to see what Eugene Stone
wrote in hers, for it does not look as smooth as it
did at first.   We have autograph albums too and
Horace Finley gave us lots of small photographs.
We paste them in the books and then ask the people
to write their names.   We have got Miss Upham's
picture and Dr. and Mrs. Daggett, General
Granger's and Hon. Francis Granger's and Mrs.
Adele Granger Thayer and Friend Burling, Dr.
Jewett, Dr. Cheney, Deacon Andrews and Dr. Carr,

and Johnnie Thompson's, Mr. Noah T. Clarke, Mr.
E. M. Morse, Mrs. George Willson, Theodore Bar-
num, Jim Paton's and Will Schley, Merritt Wilcox,
Tom Raines, Ed. Williams, Gus Coleman's, W. P.
Fisk and lots of the girls' pictures besides. Eugene
Stone and Tom Eddy had their ambrotypes taken
together, in a handsome case, and gave it to Anna.
We are going to keep them always.

April.—The Siamese twins are in town and a lot
of the girls went to see them in Bemis Hall this
afternoon. It costs 10 cents. Grandmother let us
go. Their names are Eng and Chang and they are
not very handsome. They are two men joined together. I hope they like each other but I don't envy
them any way. If one wanted to go somewhere and
the other one didn't I don't see how they would man-
age it. One would have to give up, that's certain.
Perhaps they are both Christians.

April 30.—Rev. Henry M. Field, editor of the
New York Evangelist, and his little French wife are
here visiting. She is a wonderful woman. She has
written a book and paints beautiful pictures and was
teacher of art in Cooper Institute, New York. He
is Grandmother's nephew and he brought her a picture of himself and his five brothers, taken for
Grandmother, because she is the only aunt they have
in the world. The rest are all dead. The men in
the picture are Jonathan and Matthew and David

Dudley and Stephen J. and Cyrus W. and Henry M.
They are all very nice looking and Grandmother
thinks a great deal of the picture.

May 15.—Miss Anna Gaylord is one of my teachers at the seminary and when I told her that I wrote
a journal every day she wanted me to bring her my
last book and let her read it. I did so and she said
she enjoyed it very much and she hoped I would
keep them for they would be interesting for me to
read when I am old. I think I shall do so. She has
a very particular friend, Rev. Mr. Beaumont, who is
one of the teachers at the Academy. I think they
are going to be married some day. I guess I will
show her this page of my journal, too. Grandmother let me make a pie in a saucer to-day and it
was very good.

May.—We were invited to Bessie Seymour's
party last night and Grandmother said we could go.
The girls all told us at school that they were going
to wear low neck and short sleeves. We have caps
on the sleeves of our best dresses and we tried to get
the sleeves out, so we could go bare arms, but we
couldn't get them out. We had a very nice time,
though, at the party. Some of the Academy boys
were there and they asked us to dance but of course
we couldn't do that. We promenaded around the
rooms and went out to supper with them. Eugene
Stone and Tom Eddy asked to go home with us but

"Uncle David Dudley Field"

Tom Eddy and Eugene Stone

Grandmother sent our two girls for us, Bridget
Flynn and Hannah White, so they couldn't. We
were quite disappointed, but perhaps she won't send
for us next time.

May.—Grandmother is teaching me how to knit
some mittens now, but if I ever finish them it will
be through much tribulation, the way they have to
be raveled out and commenced over again. I think
I shall know how to knit when I get through, if I
never know how to do anything else. Perhaps I
shall know how to write, too, for I write all of
Grandmother's letters for her, because it tires her to
write too much. I have sorted my letters to-day
and tied them in packages and found I had between
500 and 600. I have had about two letters a week
for the past five years and have kept them all.
Father almost always tells me in his letters to read
my Bible and say my prayers and obey Grandmother
and stand up straight and turn out my toes and
brush my teeth and be good to my little sister. I
have been practising all these so long I can say, as
the young man did in the Bible when Jesus told him
what to do to be saved, " all these have I kept from
my youth up." But then, I lack quite a number of
things after all. I am not always strictly obedient.
For instance, I know Grandmother never likes to
have us read the secular part of the *New York Ob-
server* on Sunday, so she puts it in the top drawer
of the sideboard until Monday, but I couldn't find

anything interesting to read the other Sunday so I took it out and read it and put it back. The jokes and stories in it did not seem as amusing as usual so I think I will not do it again.

Grandfather's favorite paper is the *Boston Christian Register*. He could not have one of them torn up any more than a leaf of the Bible. He has barrels of them stored away in the garret.

I asked Grandmother to-day to write a verse for me to keep always and she wrote a good one: "To be happy and live long the three grand essentials are: Be busy, love somebody and have high aims." I think, from all I have noticed about her, that she has had this for her motto all her life and I don't think Anna and I can do very much better than to try and follow it too. Grandfather tells us sometimes, when she is not in the room, that the best thing we can do is to be just as near like Grandmother as we can possibly be.

Saturday, May 30.—Louisa Field came over to dinner to-day and brought Allie with her. We had roast chickens for dinner and lots of other nice things. Grandmother taught us how to string lilac blossoms for necklaces and also how to make curls of dandelion stems. She always has some things in the parlor cupboard which she brings out on extra occasions, so she got them out to-day. They are some Chinamen which Uncle Thomas brought home when he sailed around the world. They are wooden images standing in boxes, packing tea with their feet.

Last week Jennie Howell invited us to go up to Black Point Cabin with her and to-day with a lot of grown-up people we went and enjoyed it. There was a little colored girl there who waits on the table and can row the boats too. She is Polly Carroll's grand-daughter, Mary Jane. She sang for us,

" Nellie Bly shuts her eye when she goes to sleep,
　　When she opens them again her eyes begin to peep;
　　Hi Nellie, Ho Nellie, listen love to me,
　　I'll sing for you, I'll play for you,
　　　　A dulcet melody."

She is just as cute as she can be. She said Mrs. Henry Chesebro taught her to read.

Sunday, June 1.—Rev. Dr. Shaw, of Rochester, preached for Dr. Daggett to-day and his text was: " Whosoever drinketh of this water shall thirst again, but whosoever drinketh of the water that I shall give him shall never thirst." He said by this water he meant the pleasures of this life, wealth and fame and honor, of which the more we have the more we want and are never satisfied, but if we drink of the water that Christ can give us we will have happiness here and forever. It was a very good sermon and I love to hear him preach. Grandmother never likes to start for church until after all the Seminary girls and Academy boys have

gone by, but this morning we got to the gate just
as the boys came along.   When Grandmother saw
five or six hats come off and knew they were bowing
to us, she asked us how we got acquainted with
them.   We told her that almost all the girls knew
the Academy boys and I am sure that is true.

Tuesday, June 8.—We are cleaning house now
and Grandmother asked Anna and me to take out a
few tacks in the dining-room carpet.   We did not
like it so very well but we liked eating dinner in
the parlor, as the table had to be set in there.   Anna
told us that when she got married we could come to
visit her any time in the year as she was never going
to clean house.   We went down street on an errand
to-night and hurried right back, as Grandmother
said she should look at the clock and see how long
we were gone.   Emma Wheeler went with us.
Anna says she and Emma are as "thick as hasty
pudding."

June.—Rev. Frederick Starr, of Penn Yan, had
an exhibition in Bemis Hall to-day of a tabernacle
just like the children of Israel carried with them to
the Promised Land.   We went to see it.   He made
it himself and said he took all the directions from
the Bible and knew where to put the curtains and
the poles and everything.   It was interesting but we
thought it would be queer not to have any church
to go to but one like that, that you could take down

and put up and carry around with you wherever you
went.

June.—Rev. Mr. Kendall is not going to preach
in East Bloomfield any more. The paper says he
is going to New York to live and be Secretary of
the A.B.C.F.M. I asked Grandmother what that
meant, and she said he would have to write down
what the missionaries do. I guess that will keep
him busy. Grandfather's nephew, a Mr. Adams of
Boston and his wife, visited us about two weeks ago.
He is the head of the firm Adams' Express Co.
Anna asked them if they ever heard the conundrum
" What was Eve made for? " and they said no, so
she told them the answer, " for Adam's express company." They thought it was quite good. When
they reached home, they sent us each a reticule, with
scissors, thimble, stiletto, needle-case and tiny pen-
knife and some stamped embroidery. They must
be very rich.

Saturday Night, July.—Grandfather was asking
us to-night how many things we could remember,
and I told him I could remember when Zachary Taylor died, and our church was draped in black, and
Mr. Daggett preached a funeral sermon about him,
and I could remember when Daniel Webster died,
and there was service held in the church and his last
words, " I still live," were put up over the pulpit.
He said he could remember when George Washing-

ton died and when Benjamin Franklin died. He was seven years old then and he was seventeen when Washington died. Of course his memory goes farther back than mine, but he said I did very well, considering.

July.—I have not written in my journal for several days because we have been out of town. Grandfather had to go to Victor on business and took Anna and me with him. Anna says she loves to ride on the cars as it is fun to watch the trees and fences run so. We took dinner at Dr. Ball's and came home on the evening train. Then Judge Ellsworth came over from Penn Yan to see Grandfather on business and asked if he could take us home with him and he said yes, so we went and had a splendid time and stayed two days. Stewart was at home and took us all around driving and took us to the graveyard to see our mother's grave. I copied this verse from the gravestone:

" Of gentle seeming was her form
  And the soft beaming of her radiant eye
  Was sunlight to the beauty of her face.
  Peace, sacred peace, was written on her brow
  And flowed in the low music of her voice
  Which came unto the list'ner like the tones of sooth-
      ing Autumn winds.
  Her hands were full of consolations which she scat-
      tered free to all—the poor, the sick, the sor-
      rowful."

I think she must have been exactly like Grandmother only she was 32 and Grandmother is 72.

Stewart went to prayer meeting because it was Wednesday night, and when he came home his mother asked him if he took part in the meeting. He said he did and she asked him what he said. He said he told the story of Ethan Allen, the infidel, who was dying, and his daughter asked him whose religion she should live by, his or her mother's, and he said, "Your mother's, my daughter, your mother's." This pleased Mrs. Ellsworth very much. Stewart is a great boy and you never can tell whether he is in earnest or not. It was very warm while we were gone and when we got home Anna told Grandmother she was going to put on her barege dress and take a rocking-chair and a glass of ice water and a palm leaf fan and go down cellar and sit, but Grandmother told her if she would just sit still and take a book and get her mind on something else besides the weather, she would be cool enough. Grandmother always looks as cool as a cucumber even when the thermometer is 90 in the shade.

Sunday, August.—Rev. Anson D. Eddy preached this morning. His text was from the sixth chapter of John, 44th verse. "No man can come to me, except the Father which hath sent me, draw him." He is Tom Eddy's father, and very good-looking and smart too. He used to be one of the ministers

of our church before Mr. Daggett came.   He wrote
a book in our Sunday School library, about Old
Black Jacob, and Grandmother loves to read it.
We had a nice dinner to-day, green peas, lemonade
and gooseberry pie.   We had cold roast lamb too,
because Grandmother never has any meat cooked on
Sunday.

Sunday.—Mr. Noah T. Clarke is superintendent
of our Sunday School now, and this morning he
asked, " What is prayer? "   No one answered, so I
stood up and gave the definition from the catechism.
He seemed pleased and so was Grandmother when
I told her.   Anna said she supposes she was glad
that " her labor was not in vain in the Lord."   I
think she is trying to see if she can say Bible verses,
like grown-up people do.

Grandfather said that I did better than the little
boy he read about who, when a visitor asked the
Sunday School children what was the ostensible
object of Sabbath School instruction, waited till the
question was repeated three times and then stood up
and said, " Yes, sir."

Wednesday.—We could not go to prayer meeting
to-night because it rained, so Grandmother said we
could go into the kitchen and stand by the window
and hear the Methodists.   We could hear every
word that old Father Thompson said, and every

hymn they sung, but Mr. Jervis used such big words
we could not understand him at all.

Sunday.—Grandmother says she loves to look at
the beautiful white heads of Mr. Francis Granger
and General Granger as they sit in their pews in
church. She says that is what it means in the
twelfth chapter of Ecclesiastes where it says, " And
the almond tree shall flourish." I don't know exactly why it means them, but I suppose she does.
We have got a beautiful almond tree in our front
yard covered with flowers, but the blossoms are pink.
Probably they had white ones in Jerusalem, where
Solomon lived.

Monday.—Mr. Alex. Jeffrey has come from
Lexington, Ky., and brought Mrs. Ross and his
three daughters, Julia, Shaddie and Bessie Jeffrey.
Mrs. Ross knows Grandmother and came to call
and brought the girls. They are very pretty and
General Granger's grand-daughters. I think they
are going to stay all summer.

Thanksgiving Day.—We all went to church and
Dr. Daggett's text was: " He hath not dealt so
with any nation." Aunt Glorianna and her children
were here and Uncle Field and all their family and
Dr. Carr and all his family. There were about sixteen of us in all and we children had a table in the
corner all by ourselves. We had roast turkey and

everything else we could think of. After dinner we went into the parlor and Aunt Glorianna played on the piano and sang, " Flow gently, sweet Afton, among thy green braes," and " Poor Bessie was a sailor's wife." These are Grandfather's favorites. Dr. Carr sang " I'm sitting on the stile, Mary, where we sat side by side." He is a beautiful singer. It seemed just like Sunday, for Grandmother never likes to have us work or play on Thanksgiving Day, but we had a very good time, indeed, and were sorry when they all went home.

Saturday, December 20.—Lillie Reeve and her brother, Charlie, have come from Texas to live. He goes to the Academy and she boards with Miss Antoinette Pierson. Miss Pierson invited me up to spend the afternoon and take tea with her and I went and had a very nice time. She told me about their camp life in Texas and how her mother died, and her little baby sister, Minnie, lives with her Grandmother Sheppard in Dansville. She is a very nice girl and I like her very much, indeed.

1857

January 8.—Anna and Alice Jewett caught a ride down to the lake this afternoon on a bob-sleigh, and then caught a ride back on a load of frozen pigs. In jumping off, Anna tore her flannel petticoat from the band down. I did not enjoy the situation as much as Anna, because I had to sit up after she had gone to bed, and darn it by candle light, because she was afraid Grandmother might see the rent and inquire into it, and that would put an end to bob-sled exploits.

March 6.—Anna and her set will have to square accounts with Mr. Richards to-morrow, for nine of them ran away from school this afternoon, Alice Jewett, Louisa Field, Sarah Antes, Hattie Paddock, Helen Coy, Jennie Ruckel, Frankie Younglove, Emma Wheeler and Anna. They went out to Mr. Sackett's, where they are making maple sugar. Mr. and Mrs. Sackett were at home and two Miss Sacketts and Darius, and they asked them in and gave them all the sugar they wanted, and Anna said pickles, too, and bread and butter, and the more pickles they ate the more sugar they could eat. I guess they will think of pickles when Mr. Richards asks them where they were. I think Ellie Daggett and Charlie Paddock went, too, and some of the Academy boys.

March 7.—They all had to stay after school to-night for an hour and copy Dictionary. Anna seems reconciled, for she just wrote in her journal: " It was a very good plan to keep us because no one ever ought to stay out of school except on account of sickness, and if they once get a thing fixed in their minds it will stay there, and when they grow up it will do them a great deal of good."

April.—Grandfather gave us 10 cents each this morning for learning the 46th Psalm and has promised us $1 each for reading the Bible through in a year. We were going to any way. Some of the girls say they should think we would be afraid of Grandfather, he is so sober, but we are not the least bit. He let us count $1,000 to-night which a Mr. Taylor, a cattle buyer, brought to him in the evening after banking hours. Anybody must be very rich who has all that money of their own.

Friday.—Our old horse is dead and we will have to buy another. He was very steady and faithful. One day Grandfather left him at the front gate and he started along and turned the corner all right, down the Methodist lane and went way down to our barn doors and stood there until Mr. Piser came and took him into the barn. People said they set

their clocks by him because it was always quarter
past 12 when he was driven down to the bank after
Grandfather and quarter of 1 when he came back.
I don't think the clocks would ever be too fast if
they were set by him. We asked Grandfather what
he died of and he said he had run his race but I
think he meant he had walked it, for I never saw
him go off a jog in my life. Anna used to say he
was taking a nap when we were out driving with
Grandfather. I have written some lines in his memory and if I knew where he was buried, I would
print it on his head board.

> Old Dobbin's dead, that good old horse,
>   We ne'er shall see him more,
> He always used to lag behind
>   But now he's gone before.

It is a parody on old Grimes is dead, which is in
our reader, only that is a very long poem. I am
not going to show mine to Grandfather till he gets
over feeling bad about the horse.

Sunday.—Grandmother gave Anna, Doddridge's
"Rise and Progress of Religion in the Soul" to
read to-day. Anna says she thinks she will have
to rise and progress a good deal before she will be
able to appreciate it. Baxter's "Saints Rest"
would probably suit her better.

Sunday, April 5.—An agent for the American Board of Foreign Missions preached this morning in our church from Romans 10: 15: "How shall they hear without a preacher and how shall they preach except they be sent." An agent from every society presents the cause, whatever it is, once a year and some people think the anniversary comes around very often. I always think of Mrs. George Wilson's poem on " A apele for air, pewer air, certin proper for the pews, which, she sez, is scarce as piety, or bank bills when ajents beg for mischuns, wich sum say is purty often, (taint nothin' to me, wat I give aint nothin' to nobody)." I think that is about the best poem of its kind I ever read.

Miss Lizzie Bull told us in Sunday School to-day that she cannot be our Sunday School teacher any more, as she and her sister Mary are going to join the Episcopal Church. We hate to have her go, but what can't be cured must be endured. Part of our class are going into Miss Mary Howell's class and part into Miss Annie Pierce's. They are both splendid teachers and Miss Lizzie Bull is another. We had preaching in our church this afternoon, too. Rev. Samuel Hanson Cox, of Le Roy Female Seminary, preached. He is a great man, very large, long white hair combed back. I think if a person once saw him they would never forget him. He preached about Melchisidek, who had neither " beginning of days or end of life." Some people thought that was like his sermon, for it was more than one hour

long. Dr. Cox and Mrs. Taylor came to call and
asked Grandfather to let me go to Le Roy Female
Seminary, but Grandfather likes Ontario Female
Seminary better than any other in the world. We
wanted Grandmother to have her picture taken, but
she did not feel able to go to Mr. Finley's, so he
came up Tuesday and took it in our dining-room.
She had her best cap on and her black silk dress and
sat in her high back rocking chair in her usual corner near the window. He brought one up to show
us and we like it so much. Anna looked at it and
kissed it and said, " Grandmother, I think you are
perfectly beautiful." She smiled and very modestly
put her handkerchief up to her face and said, " You
foolish child," but I am sure she was pleased, for
how could she help it? A man came up to the open
window one day where she was sitting, with something to sell, and while she was talking to him he
said, " You must have been handsome, lady, when
you were young." Grandmother said it was because he wanted to sell his wares, but we thought
he knew it was so. We told her she couldn't get
around it that way and we asked Grandfather and
he said it was true. Our Sunday School class went
to Mr. Finley's to-day and had a group ambrotype
taken for our teacher, Miss Annie Pierce; Susie
Daggett, Clara Willson, Sarah Whitney, Mary Field
and myself. Mary Wheeler ought to have been in
it, too, but we couldn't get her to come. We had
very good success.

Thursday.—We gave the ambrotype to Miss
Pierce and she liked it very much and so does her
mother and Fannie.   Her mother is lame and cannot go anywhere so we often go to see her and she
is always glad to see us and so pleasant.

May 9.—Miss Lizzie Bull came for me to go bot-
anising with her this morning and we were gone
from 9 till 12, and went clear up to the orphan asylum.   I am afraid I am not a born botanist, for all
the time she was analysing the flowers and telling
me about the corona and the corolla and the calyx
and the stamens and petals and pistils, I was thinking what beautiful hands she had and how dainty
they looked, pulling the blossoms all to pieces.   I
am afraid I am commonplace, like the man we read
of in English literature, who said " a primrose by
the river brim, a yellow primrose, was to him, and
it was nothing more."
Mr. William Wood came to call this afternoon
and gave us some morning-glory seeds to sow and
told us to write down in our journals that he did so.
So here it is.   What a funny old man he is.   Anna
and Emma Wheeler went to Hiram Tousley's
funeral to-day.   She has just written in her journal
that Hiram's corpse was very perfect of him and
that Fannie looked very pretty in black.   She also
added that after the funeral Grandfather took Aunt
Ann and Lucilla out to ride to Mr. Howe's and just
as they got there it sprinkled.   She says she don't

know "weather" they got wet or not. She went
to a picnic at Sucker Brook yesterday afternoon,
and this is the way she described it in her journal.
"Miss Hurlburt told us all to wear rubbers and
shawls and bring some cake and we would have a
picnic. We had a very warm time. It was very
warm indeed and I was most roasted and we were
all very thirsty indeed. We had in all the party
about 40 of us. It was very pleasant and I enjoyed
myself exceedingly. We had boiled eggs, pickles,
Dutch cheese and sage cheese and loaf cake and
raisin cake, pound cake, dried beef and capers, jam
and tea cakes and gingerbread, and we tried to catch
some fish but we couldn't, and in all we had a very
nice time. I forgot to say that I picked some flowers for my teacher. I went to bed tired out and
worn out."

Her next entry was the following day when she
and the other scholars dressed up to " speak pieces."
She says, " After dinner I went and put on my rope
petticoat and lace one over it and my barege de laine
dress and all my rings and white bask and breastpin
and worked handkerchief and spoke my piece. It
was, ' When I look up to yonder sky.' It is very
pretty indeed and most all the girls said I looked
nice and said it nice. They were all dressed up,
too."

Thursday.—I asked Grandfather why we do not
have gas in the house like almost every one else

and he said because it was bad for the eyes and he liked candles and sperm oil better. We have the funniest little sperm oil lamp with a shade on to read by evenings and the fire on the hearth gives Grandfather and Grandmother all the light they want, for she knits in her corner and we read aloud to them if they want us to. I think if Grandfather is proud of anything besides being a Bostonian, it is that everything in the house is forty years old. The shovel and tongs and andirons and fender and the haircloth sofa and the haircloth rocking chair and the flag bottomed chairs painted dark green and the two old arm-chairs which belong to them and no one else ever thinks of touching. There is a wooden partition between the dining-room and parlor and they say it can slide right up out of sight on pulleys, so that it would be all one room. We have often said that we wished we could see it go up but they say it has never been up since the day our mother was married and as she is dead I suppose it would make them feel bad, so we probably will always have it down. There are no curtains or even shades at the windows, because Grandfather says, " light is sweet and a pleasant thing it is to behold the sun." The piano is in the parlor and it is the same one that our mother had when she was a little girl but we like it all the better for that. There are four large oil paintings on the parlor wall, De Witt Clinton, Rev. Mr. Dwight, Uncle Henry Channing Beals and Aunt Lucilla Bates, and no matter where we sit in the

room they are watching and their eyes seem to move
whenever we do.   There is quite a handsome lamp
on a mahogany center table, but I never saw it
lighted.   We have four sperm candles in four silver
candlesticks and when we have company we light
them.   Johnnie Thompson, son of the minister,
Rev. M. L. R. P., has come to the academy to school
and he is very full of fun and got acquainted with
all the girls very quick.   He told us this afternoon
to have " the other candle lit " for he was coming
down to see us this evening.   Will Schley heard him
say it and he said he was coming too.   His mother
says she always knows when he has been at our
house, because she finds sperm on his clothes and has
to take brown paper and a hot flatiron to get it out,
but still I do not think that Mrs. Schley cares, for
she is a very nice lady and she and I are great
friends.   I presume she would just as soon he
would spend part of his time with us as to be with
Horace Finley all the time.   Those boys are just
like twins.   We never see one without being sure
that the other is not far away.

Later.—The boys came and we had a very
pleasant evening but when the 9 o'clock bell rang we
heard Grandfather winding up the clock and scrap-
ing up the ashes on the hearth to cover the fire so it
would last till morning and we all understood the
signal and they bade us good-night.   " We won't

go home till morning " is a song that will never be sung in this house.

June 2.—Abbie Clark wrote such a nice piece in my album to-day I am going to write it in my journal. Grandfather says he likes the sentiment as well as any in my book. This is it: " It has been said that the friendship of some people is like our shadow, keeping close by us while the sun shines, deserting us the moment we enter the shade, but think not such is the friendship of Abbie S. Clark." Abbie and I took supper at Miss Mary Howell's tonight to see Adele Ives. We had a lovely time.

Tuesday.—General Tom Thumb was in town today and everybody who wanted to see him could go to Bemis Hall. Twenty-five cents for old people, and 10 cents for children, but we could see him for nothing when he drove around town. He had a little carriage and two little bits of ponies and a little boy with a high silk hat on, for the driver. He sat inside the coach but we could see him looking out. We went to the hall in the afternoon and the man who brought him stood by him and looked like a giant and told us all about him. Then he asked Tom Thumb to make a speech and stood him upon the table. He told all the ladies he would give them a kiss if they would come up and buy his picture. Some of them did.

Friday, July.—I have not kept a journal for two weeks because we have been away visiting. Anna and I had an invitation to go to Utica to visit Rev. and Mrs. Brandigee. He is rector of Grace Episcopal church there and his wife used to belong to Father's church in Morristown, N. J. Her name was Miss Condict. Rev. Mr. Stowe was going to Hamilton College at Clinton, so he said he would take us to Utica. We had a lovely time. The corner stone of the church was laid while we were there and Bishop De Lancey came and stayed with us at Mr. Brandigee's. He is a very nice man and likes children. One morning they had muffins for breakfast and Anna asked if they were ragamuffins. Mr. Brandigee said, " Yes, they are made of rags and brown paper," but we knew he was just joking. When we came away Mrs. Brandigee gave me a prayer book and Anna a vase, but she didn't like it and said she should tell Mrs. Brandigee she wanted a prayer book too, so I had to change with her. When we came home Mr. Brandigee put us in care of the conductor. There was a fine soldier looking man in the car with us and we thought it was his wife with him. He wore a blue coat and brass buttons, and some one said his name was Custer and that he was a West Point cadet and belonged to the regular army. I told Anna she had better behave or he would see her, but she would go out and stand on the platform until the conductor told her not to. I pulled her dress and looked very stern at

her and motioned toward Mr. Custer, but it did not
seem to have any impression on her. I saw Mr.
Custer smile once because my words had no effect.
I was glad when we got to Canandaigua. I heard
some one say that Dr. Jewett was at the depôt to
take Mr. Custer and his wife to his house, but I only
saw Grandfather coming after us. He said, " Well,
girls, you have been and you have got back," but I
could see that he was glad to have us at home again,
even if we are " troublesome comforts," as he sometimes says.

July 4.—Barnum's circus was in town to-day and
if Grandmother had not seen the pictures on the
hand bills I think she would have let us go. She
said it was all right to look at the creatures God had
made but she did not think He ever intended that
women should go only half dressed and stand up and
ride on horses bare back, or jump through hoops in
the air. So we could not go. We saw the street
parade though and heard the band play and saw the
men and women in a chariot, all dressed so fine, and
we saw a big elephant and a little one and a camel
with an awful hump on his back, and we could hear
the lion roar in the cage, as they went by. It must
have been nice to see them close to and probably we
will some day.

August 8.—Grandfather has given me his whole
set of Waverley novels and his whole set of Shake-

Grandmother's Rocking Chair   The Grandfather Clock

speare's plays, and has ordered Mr. Jahn, the cabi-
netmaker, to make me a black walnut bookcase, with
glass doors and three deep drawers underneath,
with brass handles. He is so good. Anna says
perhaps he thinks I am going to be married and go
to housekeeping some day. Well, perhaps he does.
Stranger things have happened. " Barkis is will-
in'," and I always like to please Grandfather. I
have just read David Copperfield and was so interested I could not leave it alone till I finished it.

September 1.—Anna and I have been in Litch-
field, Conn., at Father's school for boys. It is kept
in the old Beecher house, where Dr. Lyman Beecher
lived. We went up into the attic, which is light and
airy, where they say he used to write his famous sermons. James is one of the teachers and he came
for us. We went to Farmington and saw all the
Cowles families, as they are our cousins. Then we
drove by the Charter Oak and saw all there is left
of it. It was blown down last year but the stump
is fenced around. In Hartford we visited Gallau-
det's Institution for the deaf and dumb and went to
the historical rooms, where we saw some of George
Washington's clothes and his watch and his pen-
knife, but we did not see his little hatchet. We
stayed two weeks in New York and vicinity before
we came home. Uncle Edward took us to Christie's
Minstrels and the Hippodrome, so we saw all the
things we missed seeing when the circus was here in

town. Grandmother seemed surprised when we told her, but she didn't say much because she was so glad to have us at home again.   Anna said we ought to bring a present to Grandfather and Grandmother, for she read one time about some children who went away and came back grown up and brought home " busts of the old philosophers for the sitting-room," so as we saw some busts of George Washington and Benjamin Franklin in plaster of paris we bought them, for they look almost like marble and Grandfather and Grandmother like them.   Speaking of busts reminds me of a conundrum I heard while I was gone.   " How do we know that Poe's Raven was a dissipated bird?   Because he was all night on a bust."   Grandfather took us down to the bank to see how he had it made over while we were gone. We asked him why he had a beehive hanging out for a sign and he said, " Bees store their honey in the summer for winter use and men ought to store their money against a rainy day."   He has a swing door to the bank with " Push " on it.   He said he saw a man studying it one day and finally looking up he spelled p-u-s-h, push (and pronounced it like mush). " What does that mean? "   Grandfather showed him what it meant and he thought it was very convenient.   He was about as thick-headed as the man who saw some snuffers and asked what they were for and when told to snuff the candle with, he immediately snuffed the candle with his fingers and put it in the snuffers and said, " Law sakes, how handy! "

Grandmother really laughed when she read this in the paper.

September.—Mrs. Martin, of Albany, is visiting Aunt Ann, and she brought Grandmother a fine fish that was caught in the Atlantic Ocean. We went over and asked her to come to dinner to-morrow and help eat it and she said if it did not rain pitchforks she would come, so I think we may expect her. Her granddaughter, Hattie Blanchard, has come here to go to the seminary and will live with Aunt Ann. She is a very pretty girl. Mary Field came over this morning and we went down street together. Grandfather went with us to Mr. Nat Gorham's store, as he is selling off at cost, and got Grandmother and me each a new pair of kid gloves. Hers are black and mine are green. Hers cost six shillings and mine cost five shillings and six pence; very cheap for such nice ones. Grandmother let Anna have six little girls here to supper to-night: Louisa Field, Hattie Paddock, Helen Coy, Martha Densmore, Emma Wheeler and Alice Jewett. We had a splendid supper and then we played cards. I do not mean regular cards, mercy no! Grandfather thinks those kind are contagious or outrageous or something dreadful and never keeps them in the house. Grandmother said they found a pack once, when the hired man's room was cleaned, and they went into the fire pretty quick. The kind we played was just " Dr. Busby," and another " The Old Soldier

and His Dog." There are counters with them, and
if you don't have the card called for you have to
pay one into the pool. It is real fun. They all said
they had a very nice time, indeed, when they bade
Grandmother good-night, and said: " Mrs. Beals,
you must let Carrie and Anna come and see us some
time," and she said she would. I think it is nice to
have company.

Christmas.—Grandfather and Grandmother do
not care much about making Christmas presents.
They say, when they were young no one observed
Christmas or New Years, but they always kept
Thanksgiving day. Our cousins, the Fields and
Carrs, gave us several presents and Uncle Edward
sent us a basket full from New York by express.
Aunt Ann gave me one of the Lucy books and a
Franconia story book and to Anna, " The Child's
Book on Repentance." When Anna saw the title,
she whispered to me and said if she had done anything she was sorry for she was willing to be for-
given. I am afraid she will never read hers but I
will lend her mine. Miss Lucy Ellen Guernsey, of
Rochester, gave me " Christmas Earnings " and
wrote in it, " Carrie C. Richards with the love of
the author." I think that is very nice. Anna and
I were chattering like two magpies to-day, and a
man came in to talk to Grandfather on business.
He told us in an undertone that children should be
seen and not heard. After he had gone I saw Anna

watching him a long time till he was only a speck in
the distance and I asked her what she was doing.
She said she was doing it because it was a sign if
you watched persons out of sight you would never
see them again.　She does not seem to have a very
forgiving spirit, but you can't always tell.

Mr. William Wood, the venerable philanthropist
of whom Canandaigua has been justly proud for
many years, is dead.　I have preserved this poem,
written by Mrs. George Willson in his honor:

" MR. EDITOR—The following lines were written by
a lady of this village, and have been heretofore published, but on reading in your last paper the interesting extract relating to the late William Wood, Esq.,
it was suggested that they be again published, not
only for their merit, but also to keep alive the memory
of one who has done so much to ornament our village.—H."

When first on this stage of existence we come
Blind, deaf, puny, helpless, but not, alas, dumb,
What can please us, and soothe us, and make us sleep
　　good?
To be rocked in a cradle;—and cradles are wood.

When older we grow, and we enter the schools
Where masters break rulers o'er boys who break rules,
What can curb and restrain and make laws understood
But the birch-twig and ferule?—and both are of wood.

When old age—second childhood, takes vigor away,
And we totter along toward our home in the clay,

What can aid us to stand as in manhood we stood
But our tried, trusty staff?—and the staff is of wood.

And when from this stage of existence we go,
And death drops the curtain on all scenes below,
In our coffins we rest, while for worms we are food,
And our last sleeping place, like our first, is of wood.

Then honor to wood! fresh and strong may it grow,
'Though winter has silvered its summit with snow;
Embowered in its shade long our village has stood;
She'd scarce be Canandaigua if stripped of her Wood.

Stanza added after the death of Mr. Wood

The sad time is come; she is stript of her Wood,
'Though the trees that he planted still stand where they
    stood,
Still with storms they can wrestle with arms stout and
    brave;
Still they wave o'er our dwellings—they droop o'er his
    grave!
Alas! that the life of the cherished and good
Is more frail and more brief than the trees of the
    wood!

1858

February 24, 1858.—The boarders at the Seminary had some tableaux last evening and invited a great many from the village. As we went in with the crowd, we heard some one say, " Are they going to have tableaux? Well, I thought I smelt them!" They were splendid. Mr. Chubbuck was in nearly all of them. The most beautiful one was Abraham offering up Isaac. Mr. Chubbuck was Abraham and Sarah Ripley was Isaac. After the tableaux they acted a charade. The word was " Masterpiece." It was fine. After the audience got half way out of the chapel Mr. Richards announced " The Belle of the Evening." The curtain rose and every one rushed back, expecting to see a young lady dressed in the height of fashion, when immediately the Seminary bell rang! Mr. Blessner's scholars gave all the music and he stamped so, beating time, it almost drowned the music. Some one suggested a bread and milk poultice for his foot. Anna has been taking part in some private theatricals. The play is in contrast to " The Spirit of '76 " and the idea carried out is that the men should stay at home and rock the cradles and the women should take the rostrum. Grandmother was rather opposed to the idea, but every one wanted Anna to take the part of

leading lady, so she consented. She even helped
Anna make her bloomer suit and sewed on the braid
for trimming on the skirt herself. She did not
know that Anna's opening sentence was, " How are
you, sir? Cigar, please! " It was acted at Mrs.
John Bates' house on Gibson Street and was a great
success, but when they decided to repeat it another
evening Grandmother told Anna she must choose between going on the stage and living with her Grandmother, so Anna gave it up and some one else took
her part.

March.—There is a great deal said about spirits
nowadays and a lot of us girls went into one of the
recitation rooms after school to-night and had a
spiritual seance. We sat around Mr. Chubbuck's
table and put our hands on it and it moved around
and stood on two legs and sometimes on one. I
thought the girls helped it but they said they didn't.
We heard some loud raps, too, but they sounded
very earthly to me. Eliza Burns, one of the boarders, told us if we would hold our breath we could
pick up one of the girls from the floor and raise her
up over our heads with one finger of each hand, if
the girl held her breath, too. We tried it with
Anna and did it, but we had such hard work to keep
from laughing I expected we would drop her.
There is nothing very spirituelle about any of us.
I told Grandmother and she said we reminded her of
Jemima Wilkinson, who told all her followers that

the world was to come to an end on a certain day
and they should all be dressed in white and get up
on the roofs of the houses and be prepared to ascend
and meet the Lord in the air.   I asked Grandmother
what she said when nothing happened and she said
she told them it was because they did not have faith
enough.   If they had, everything would have happened just as she said.   Grandmother says that one
day at a time has always been enough for her and
that to-morrow will take care of the things of itself.

May, 1858.—Several of us girls went up into the
top of the new Court House to-day as far as the
workmen would allow us.   We got a splendid view
of the lake and of all the country round.   Abbie
Clark climbed up on a beam and recited part of
Alexander Selkirk's soliloquy:

> " I'm monarch of all I survey,
>   My rights there are none to dispute:
> From the center, all round to the sea,
>   I'm lord of the fowl and brute."

I was standing on a block and she said I looked
like " Patience on a monument smiling at Grief."   I
am sure she could not be taken for " Grief."   She
always has some quotation on her tongue's end.
We were down at Sucker Brook the other day and
she picked her way out to a big stone in the middle
of the stream and, standing on it, said, in the words
of Rhoderick Dhu,

" Come one, come all, this rock shall fly
From its firm base, as soon as I."

Just then the big stone tipped over and she had
to wade ashore.   She is not at all afraid of climbing
and as we left the Court House she said she would
like to go outside on the cupola and help Justice bal-
ance the scales.

A funny old man came to our house to-day as he
wanted to deposit some money and reached the bank
after it was closed.   We were just sitting down to
dinner so Grandfather asked him to stay and have
" pot luck " with us.   He said that he was very
much " obleeged " and stayed and passed his plate
a second time for more of our very fine " pot luck."
We had boiled beef and dumplings and I suppose he
thought that was the name of the dish.   He talked
so queer we couldn't help noticing it.   He said he
" heered " so and he was " afeered " and somebody
was very " deef " and they " hadn't ought to have
done it " and " they should have went " and such
things.   Anna and I almost laughed but Grandmother looked at us with her eye and forefinger so
we sobered down.   She told us afterwards that
there are many good people in the world whose
verbs and nouns do not agree, and instead of laughing at them we should be sure that we always speak
correctly ourselves.   Very true.   Dr. Daggett was
at the Seminary one day when we had public exercises and he told me afterwards that I said

"sagac-ious" for "saga-cious" and Aunt Ann told me that I said "epi-tome" for "e-pit-o-me." So "people that live in glass houses shouldn't throw stones."

Sunday.—Grandfather read his favorite parable this morning at prayers—the one about the wise man who built his house upon a rock and the foolish man who built upon the sand. He reads it good, just like a minister. He prays good, too, and I know his prayer by heart. He says, "Verily Thou art our Father, though Abraham be ignorant of us and Israel acknowledge us not," and he always says, "Thine arm is not shortened that it cannot save, or Thine ear heavy that it cannot hear." I am glad that I can remember it.

June.—Cyrus W. Field called at our house to-day. He is making a trip through the States and stopped here a few hours because Grandmother is his aunt. He made her a present of a piece of the Atlantic cable about six inches long, which he had mounted for her. It is a very nice souvenir. He is a tall, fine looking man and very pleasant.

Sunday, July 4, 1858.—This is Communion Sunday and quite a number united with the church on profession of their faith. Mr. Gideon Granger was one of them. Grandmother says that she has known him always and his father and mother, and

she thinks he is like John, the beloved disciple. I
think that any one who knows him, knows what is
meant by a gentle-man. I have a picture of Christ
in the Temple with the doctors, and His face is
almost exactly like Mr. Granger's. Some others
who joined to-day were Miss Belle Paton, Miss Lottie Clark and Clara Willson, Mary Wheeler and
Sarah Andrews. Dr. Daggett always asks all the
communicants to sit in the body pews and the non-
communicants in the side pews. We always feel
like the goats on the left when we leave Grandfather
and Grandmother and go on the side, but we won't
have to always. Abbie Clark, Mary Field and I
think we will join at the communion in September.
Grandmother says she hopes we realize what a solemn thing it is. We are fifteen years old so I think
we ought to. No one who hears Dr. Daggett say
in his beautiful voice, " I now renounce all ways of
sin as what I truly abhor and choose the service of
God as my greatest privilege," could think it any
trifling matter. I feel as though I couldn't be bad
if I wanted to be, and when he blesses them and
says, " May the God of the Everlasting Covenant
keep you firm and holy to the end through Jesus
Christ our Lord," everything seems complete. He
always says at the close, " And when they had sung
an hymn they went out into the Mount of Olives."
Then he gives out the hymn, beginning:

" According to Thy gracious word,
    In deep humility,

Mr. Gideon Granger

Hon. Francis Granger

This will I do, my dying Lord
I will remember Thee."

And the last verse:

" And when these failing lips grow dumb,
And mind and memory flee,
When in Thy kingdom Thou shalt come,
Jesus remember me."

Deacon Taylor always starts the hymn. Deacon
Taylor and Deacon Tyler sit on one side of Dr.
Daggett and Deacon Clarke and Deacon Castle on
the other. Grandfather and Grandmother joined
the church fifty-one years ago and are the oldest
living members. She says they have always been
glad that they took this step when they were young.

August 17.—There was a celebration in town
to-day because the Queen's message was received on
the Atlantic cable. Guns were fired and church
bells rung and flags were waving everywhere. In
the evening there was a torchlight procession and the
town was all lighted up except Gibson Street. Allie
Antes died this morning, so the people on that street
kept their houses as usual. Anna says that probably Allie Antes was better prepared to die than any
other little girl in town. Atwater hall and the
academy and the hotel were more brilliantly illumi-
nated than any other buildings. Grandfather saw
something in a Boston paper that a minister said

in his sermon about the Atlantic cable and he
wants me to write it down in my journal. This is
it: "The two hemispheres are now successfully
united by means of the electric wire, but what is it,
after all, compared with the instantaneous communication between the Throne of Divine Grace and the
heart of man? Offer up your silent petition. It is
transmitted through realms of unmeasured space
more rapidly than the lightning's flash, and the
answer reaches the soul e're the prayer has died
away on the sinner's lips. Yet this telegraph, performing its saving functions ever since Christ died
for men on Calvary, fills not the world with exulta-
tion and shouts of gladness, with illuminations and
bonfires and the booming of cannon. The reason
is, one is the telegraph of this world and may pro-
duce revolutions on earth; the other is the sweet
communication between Christ and the Christian
soul and will secure a glorious immortality in
Heaven." Grandfather appreciates anything like
that and I like to please him.

Grandfather says he thinks the 19th Psalm is a
prophecy of the electric telegraph. "Their line
is gone out through all the earth and their words to
the end of the world." It certainly sounds like it.

Sunday.—Rev. Henry Ward Beecher is staying
at Judge Taylor's and came with them to church
to-day. Everybody knew that he was here and
thought he would preach and the church was packed

full. When he came in he went right to Judge
Taylor's pew and sat with him and did not preach
at all, but it was something to look at him. Mr.
Daggett was away on his vacation and Rev. Mr.
Jervis of the M. E. church preached. I heard some
people say they guessed even Mr. Beecher heard
some new words to-day, for Mr. Jervis is quite a
hand to make them up or find very long hard ones
in the dictionary.

August 30, 1858.—Rev. Mr. Tousley was hurt
to-day by the falling of his barn which was being
moved, and they think his back is broken and if he
lives he can never sit up again. Only last Sunday
he was in Sunday School and had us sing in memory of Allie Antes:

> " A mourning class, a vacant seat,
>   Tell us that one we loved to meet
>   Will join our youthful throng no more,
>   'Till all these changing scenes are o'er."

And now he will never meet with us again and the
children will never have another minister all their
own. He thinks he may be able to write letters to
the children and perhaps write his own life. We all
hope he may be able to sit up if he cannot walk.

We went to our old home in Penn Yan visiting
last week and stayed at Judge Ellsworth's. We
called to see the Tunnicliffs and the Olivers, Wells,
Jones, Shepards, Glovers, Bennetts, Judds and sev-

eral other families. They were glad to see us for the sake of our father and mother. Father was their pastor from 1841 to 1847.

Some one told us that when Bob and Henry Antes were small boys they thought they would like to try, just for once, to see how it would seem to be bad, so in spite of all of Mr. Tousley's sermons they went out behind the barn one day and in a whisper Bob said, " I swear," and Henry said, " So do I." Then they came into the house looking guilty and quite surprised, I suppose, that they were not struck dead just as Ananias and Sapphira were for lying.

September.—I read in a New York paper to-day that Hon. George Peabody, of England, presented Cyrus W. Field with a solid silver tea service of twelve pieces, which cost $4,000. The pieces bear likenesses of Mr. Peabody and Mr. Field, with the coat of arms of the Field family. The epergne is supported by a base representing the genius of America.

We had experiments in the philosophy class to-day and took electric shocks. Mr. Chubbuck managed the battery which has two handles attached. Two of the girls each held one of these and we all took hold of hands making the circuit complete. After a while it jerked us almost to pieces and we asked Mr. Chubbuck to turn it off. Dana Luther, one of the Academy boys, walked up from the Post-office with me this noon.   He lives in Naples and is Florence Younglove's cousin.   We went to a ball game down on Pleasant Street after school.   I got so far ahead of Anna coming home she called me her " distant relative."

1859

January, 1859.—Mr. Woodruff came to see Grandfather to ask him if we could attend his singing school. He is going to have it one evening each week in the chapel of our church. Quite a lot of the boys and girls are going, so we were glad when Grandfather gave his consent. Mr. Woodruff wants us all to sing by note and teaches " do re me fa sol la si do " from the blackboard and beats time with a stick. He lets us have a recess, which is more fun than all the rest of it. He says if we practise well we can have a concert in Bemis Hall to end up with. What a treat that will be!

February.—Anna has been teasing me all the morning about a verse which John Albert Granger Barker wrote in my album. He has a most fascinating lisp when he talks, so she says this is the way the verse reads:

> " Beauty of perthon, ith thertainly chawming
> Beauty of feachure, by no meanth alawming
> But give me in pwefrence, beauty of mind,
> Or give me Cawwie, with all thwee combined."

It takes Anna to find " amuthement " in " evewything."

Mary Wheeler came over and pierced my ears to-day, so I can wear my new earrings that Uncle Edward sent me. She pinched my ear until it was numb and then pulled a needle through, threaded with silk. Anna would not stay in the room. She wants her's done but does not dare. It is all the fashion for girls to cut off their hair and friz it. Anna and I have cut off ours and Bessie Seymour got me to cut off her lovely long hair to-day. It won't be very comfortable for us to sleep with curl papers all over our heads, but we must do it now. I wanted my new dress waist which Miss Rosewarne is making, to hook up in front, but Grandmother said I would have to wear it that way all the rest of my life so I had better be content to hook it in the back a little longer. She said when Aunt Glorianna was married, in 1848, it was the fashion for grown up women to have their waists fastened in the back, so the bride had hers made that way but she thought it was a very foolish and inconvenient fashion. It is nice, though, to dress in style and look like other people. I have a Garibaldi waist and a Zouave jacket and a balmoral skirt.

Sunday.—I asked Grandmother if I could write a letter to Father to-day, and she said I could begin it and tell him that I went to church and what Mr. Daggett's text was and then finish it to-morrow. I did so, but I wish I could do it all after I began. She said a verse from the Tract Primer:

" A Sabbath well spent brings a week of content
  And strength for the toil of to-morrow,
But a Sabbath profaned, whatever be gained,
  Is a certain forerunner of sorrow."

Monday.—We dressed up in new fangled costumes to-day and wore them to school. Some of us wore dresses almost up to our knees and some wore them trailing on the ground. Some wore their hair twisted in knots and some let theirs hang down their backs. I wore my new waterfall for the first time and Abbie Clark said I looked like " Hagar in the Wilderness." When she came in she looked like a fashion plate, bedecked with bows and ribbons and her hair up in a new way. When she came in the door she stopped and said solemnly: " If you have tears prepare to shed them now ! " Laura Chapin would not participate in the fun, for once. She said she thought " Beauty unadorned was the dorndest." We did not have our lesson in mental philosophy very well so we asked Mr. Richards to explain the nature of dreams and their cause and effect. He gave us a very interesting talk, which occupied the whole hour. We listened with breathless attention, so he must have marked us 100.

There was a lecture at the seminary to-night and Rev. Dr. Hibbard, the Methodist minister, who lives next door above the Methodist church, came home with us. Grandmother was very much pleased when we told her.

March 1.—Our hired man has started a hot bed and we went down behind the barn to see it. Grandfather said he was up at 6 o'clock and walked up as far as Mr. Greig's lions and back again for exercise before breakfast. He seems to have the bloom of youth on his face as a reward. Anna says she saw " Bloom of youth " advertised in the drug store and she is going to buy some. I know Grandmother won't let her for it would be like " taking coal to Newcastle."

April.—Anna wanted me to help her write a composition last night, and we decided to write on " Old Journals," so we got hers and mine both out and made selections and then she copied them. When we were on our way to school this morning we met Mr. E. M. Morse and Anna asked him if he did not want to read her composition that Carrie wrote for her. He made a very long face and pretended to be much shocked, but said he would like to read it, so he took it and also her album, which she asked him to write in. At night, on his way home, he stopped at our door and left them both. When she looked in her album, she found this was what he had written:

" Anna, when you have grown old and wear spectacles and a cap, remember the boyish young man who saw your fine talents in 1859 and was certain you would add culture to nature and become the pride of Canandaigua. Do not forget also that no one deserves praise for anything done by others and that your

progress in wisdom and goodness will be watched by
no one more anxiously than by your true friend,

E. M. Morse."

I think she might as well have told Mr. Morse
that the old journals were as much hers as mine;
but I think she likes to make out she is not as good
as she is. Sarah Foster helped us to do our arithmetic examples to-day. She is splendid in mathe-
matics.

Much to our surprise Bridget Flynn, who has
lived with us so long, is married. We didn't know
she thought of such a thing, but she has gone.
Anna and I have learned how to make rice and corn-
starch puddings. We have a new girl in Bridget's
place but I don't think she will do. Grandmother
asked her to-day if she seasoned the gravy and she
said, either she did or she didn't, she couldn't tell
which. Grandfather says he thinks she is a little
lacking in the " upper story."

June.—A lot of us went down to Sucker Brook
this afternoon. Abbie Clark was one and she told
us some games to play sitting down on the grass.
We played " Simon says thumbs up " and then we
pulled the leaves off from daisies and said,

" Rich man, poor man, beggar man, thief,
    Doctor, lawyer, merchant, chief,"

to see which we would marry. The last leaf tells
the story. Anna's came " rich man " every time

and she thinks it is true because Eugene Stone has asked to marry her and he is quite well off. She is 13 and he is 17. He is going now to his home in St. Paul, Minn., but he is coming back for her some day. Tom Eddy is going to be groomsman and Emma Wheeler bridesmaid. They have all the arrangements made. She has not shown any of Eugene Stone's notes to Grandmother yet for she does not think it is worth while. Anna broke the seal on Tom Eddy's page in her mystic book, although he wrote on it, " Not to be opened until December 8, 1859." He says:

" DEAR ANNA,—I hope that in a few years I will see you and Stone living on the banks of the Mississippi, in a little cottage, as snug as a bug in a rug, living in peace, so that I can come and see you and have a good time.—Yours,
THOS. C. EDDY."

Anna says if she does marry Eugene Stone and he forgets, after two or three years to be as polite to her as he is now she shall look up at him with her sweetest smile and say, " Miss Anna, won't you have a little more sugar in your tea? " When I went to school this morning Juliet Ripley asked, " Where do you think Anna Richards is now? Up in a cherry tree in Dr. Cheney's garden." Anna loves cherries. We could see her from the chapel window.

June 7.—Alice Jewett took Anna all through their new house to-day which is being built and then they went over to Mr. Noah T. Clarke's partly finished house and went all through that. A dog came out of Cat Alley and barked at them and scared Anna awfully. She said she almost had a conniption fit but Emma kept hold of her. She is so afraid of thunder and lightning and dogs.

Old Friend Burling brought Grandfather a specimen of his handwriting to-day to keep. It is beautifully written, like copper plate. This is the verse he wrote and Grandfather gave it to me to paste in my book of extracts:

DIVINE LOVE.

Could we with ink the ocean fill,
   Was the whole earth of parchment made,
Was every single stick a quill,
   And every man a scribe by trade;
To write the love of God above
   Would drain the ocean dry;
Nor could that scroll contain the whole
   Though stretched from sky to sky.

Transcribed by William S. Burling, Canandaigua, 1859, in the 83rd year of his age.

Sunday, December 8, 1859.—Mr. E. M. Morse is our Sunday School teacher now and the Sunday School room is so crowded that we go up into the church for our class recitation. Abbie Clark, Fan-

nie Gaylord and myself are the only scholars, and
he calls us the three christian graces, faith, hope and
charity, and the greatest of these is charity. I am
the tallest, so he says I am charity. We recite in
Mr. Gibson's pew, because it is farthest away and
we do not disturb the other classes. He gave us
some excellent advice to-day as to what was right
and said if we ever had any doubts about anything
we should never do it and should always be perfectly
sure we are in the right before we act. He gave us
two weeks ago a poem to learn by Samuel Taylor
Coleridge. It is an apostrophe to God and very
hard to learn. It is blank verse and has 85 lines
in it. I have it committed at last and we are to
recite it in concert. The last two lines are, " Tell
thou the silent sky and tell the stars and tell yon
rising sun, Earth with its thousand voices praises
God." Mr. Morse delivered a lecture in Bemis Hall
last Thursday night. The subject was, " You and
I." It was splendid and he lent me the manuscript
afterwards to read. Dick Valentine lectured in the
hall the other night too. His subject was " Prejudice." There was some difference in the lectures
and the lecturers. The latter was more highly colored.

Friday.—The older ladies of the town have
formed a society for the relief of the poor and are
going to have a course of lectures in Bemis Hall
under their auspices to raise funds. The lecturers

are to be from the village and are to be: Rev. O.
E. Daggett, subject, "Ladies and Gentlemen"; Dr.
Harvey Jewett, "The House We Live In"; Prof.
F. E. R. Chubbuck, "Progress"; Hon. H. W. Taylor, "The Empty Place"; Prof. E. G. Tyler,
"Finance"; Mr. N. T. Clark, "Chemistry"; E. M.
Morse, "Graybeard and His Dogmas." The young
ladies have started a society, too, and we have great
fun and fine suppers. We met at Jennie Howell's
to organize. We are to meet once in two weeks and
are to present each member with an album bed quilt
with all our names on when they are married.
Susie Daggett says she is never going to be married,
but we must make her a quilt just the same. Laura
Chapin sang, "Mary Lindsey, Dear," and we got
to laughing so that Susie Daggett and I lost our
equilibrium entirely, but I found mine by the time
I got home. Yesterday afternoon Grandfather
asked us if we did not want to go to ride with him
in the big two seated covered carriage which he does
not get out very often. We said yes, and he stopped
for Miss Hannah Upham and took her with us.
She sat on the back seat with me and we rode clear
to Farmington and kept up a brisk conversation all
the way. She told us how she became lady principal of the Ontario Female Seminary in 1830. She
was still telling us about it when we got back home.

December 23.—We have had a Christmas tree
and many other attractions in Seminary chapel.

The day scholars and townspeople were permitted to participate and we had a post office and received letters from our friends. Mr. E. M. Morse wrote me a fictitious one, claiming to be written from the north pole ten years hence. I will copy it in my journal for I may lose the letter. I had some gifts on the Christmas tree and gave some. I presented my teacher, Mr. Chubbuck, with two large hemstitched handkerchiefs with his initials embroidered in a corner of each. As he is favored with the euphonious name of Frank Emery Robinson Chubbuck it was a work of art to make his initials look beautiful. I inclosed a stanza in rhyme:

> Amid the changing scenes of life
> If any storm should rise,
> May you ever have a handkerchief
> To wipe your weeping eyes.

Here is Mr. Morse's letter:

"NORTH POLE, 10 *January* 1869.
"MISS CARRIE RICHARDS,
"MY DEAR YOUNG FRIEND.—It is very cold here and the pole is covered with ice. I climbed it yesterday to take an observation and arrange our flag, the Stars and Stripes, which I hoisted immediately on my arrival here, ten years ago. I thought I should freeze and the pole was so slippery that I was in great danger of coming down faster than was comfortable. Although this pole has been used for more than 6,000 years it is still as good as new. The works of the Great Architect do not wear out. It is now ten years

since I have seen you and my other two Christian
Graces and I have no doubt of your present position
among the most brilliant, noble and excellent women
in all America. I always knew and recognized your
great abilities. Nature was very generous to you all
and you were enjoying fine advantages at the time
I last knew you. I thought your residence with your
Grandparents an admirable school for you, and you
and your sister were most evidently the best joy of
their old age. You certainly owe much to them. At
the time that I left my three Christian Graces, Mrs.
Grundy was sometimes malicious enough to say that
they were injuring themselves by flirting. I always
told the old lady that I had the utmost confidence in
the judgment and discretion of my pupils and that
they would be very careful and prudent in all their
conduct. I confessed that flirting was wrong and
very injurious to any one who was guilty of it, but
I was very sure that you were not. I could not believe
that you would disappoint us all and become only
ordinary women, but that you would become the most
exalted characters, scorning all things unworthy of
ladies and Christians and I was right and Mrs. Grundy
was wrong. When the ice around the pole thaws out
I shall make a flying visit to Canandaigua. I send
you a tame polar bear for a playfellow. This letter
will be conveyed to you by Esquimaux express.—
Most truly yours,   E. M. MORSE."

I think some one must have shown some verses
that we girls wrote, to Mrs. Grundy and made her
think that our minds were more upon the young
men than they were upon our studies, but if people
knew how much time we spent on Paley's " Evi-

dences of Christianity " and Butler's Analogy and Kames' Elements of Criticism and Tytler's Ancient History and Olmstead's Mathematical Astronomy and our French and Latin and arithmetic and algebra and geometry and trigonometry and bookkeeping, they would know we had very little time to think of the masculine gender.

1860

New Year's Day.—We felt quite grown up to-day and not a little scared when we saw Mr. Morse and Mr. Wells and Mr. Mason and Mr. Chubbuck all coming in together to make a New Year's call. They made a tour of the town. We did not feel so flustrated when Will Schley and Horace Finley came in later. Mr. Oliver Phelps, Jr., came to call upon Grandmother. Grandfather made a few calls, too.

January 5.—Abbie Clark and I went up to see Miss Emma Morse because it is her birthday. We call her sweet Miss Emma and we think Mr. Manning Wells does, too. We went to William Wirt Howe's lecture in Bemis Hall this evening. He is a very smart young man.

Anna wanted to walk down a little ways with the girls after school so she crouched down between Helen Coy and Hattie Paddock and walked past the house. Grandmother always sits in the front window, so when Anna came in she asked her if she had to stay after school and Anna gave her an evasive answer. It reminds me of a story I read, of a lady who told the servant girl if any one called to give an evasive answer as she did not wish to

receive calls that day. By and by the door bell
rang and the servant went to the door. When she
came back the lady asked her how she dismissed the
visitor. She said, " Shure ye towld me to give an
evasive answer, so when the man asked if the lady
of the house was at home I said, ' Faith! is your
grandmother a monkey!'" We never say anything
like that to our " dear little lady," but we just change
the subject and divert the conversation into a more
agreeable channel. To-day some one came to see
Grandmother when we were gone and told her that
Anna and some others ran away from school.
Grandmother told Anna she hoped she would never
let any one bring her such a report again. Anna
said she would not, if she could possibly help it!
I wonder who it was. Some one who believes in
the text, " Look not every man on his own things,
but every man also on the things of others."
Grandfather told us to-night that we ought to be
very careful what we do as we are making history
every day. Anna says she shall try not to have hers
as dry as some that she had to learn at school to-day.

February 9.—Dear Miss Mary Howell was married to-day to Mr. Worthington, of Cincinnati.

February 28.—Grandfather asked me to read
Abraham Lincoln's speech aloud which he delivered
in Cooper Institute, New York, last evening, under
the auspices of the Republican Club. He was

escorted to the platform by David Dudley Field and introduced by William Cullen Bryant. The *New York Times* called him " a noted political exhorter and Prairie orator." It was a thrilling talk and must have stirred men's souls.

April 1.—Aunt Ann was over to see us yesterday and she said she made a visit the day before out at Mrs. William Gorham's. Mrs. Phelps and Miss Eliza Chapin also went and they enjoyed talking over old times when they were young. Maggie Gorham is going to be married on the 25th to Mr. Benedict of New York. She always said she would not marry a farmer and would not live in a cobble-stone house and now she is going to do both, for Mr. Benedict has bought the farm near theirs and it has a cobblestone house. We have always thought her one of the jolliest and prettiest of the older set of young ladies.

June.—James writes that he has seen the Prince of Wales in New York. He was up on the roof of the Continental Fire Insurance building, out on the cornice, and looked down on the procession. After-wards there was a reception for the Prince at the University Law School and James saw him close by. He says he has a very pleasant youthful face. There was a ball given for him one evening in the Academy of Music and there were 3,000 present. The ladies who danced with him will never forget it. They say that he enters into every diversion which is offered to him with the greatest tact and good nature, and when he visited Mount Vernon he showed great reverence for the memory of George Washington. He attended a literary entertainment in Boston, where Longfellow, Holmes, Emerson, Thoreau, and other Americans of distinction were presented to him. He will always be a favorite in America.

June.—Mrs. Annie Granger asked Anna and me to come over to her house and see her baby. We were very eager to go and wanted to hold it and carry it around the room. She was willing but asked us if we had any pins on us anywhere. She said she had the nurse sew the baby's clothes on every morning so that if she cried she would know whether it was pains or pins. We said we had no pins on us, so we stayed quite a while and held little Miss Hattie to our heart's content. She is named for her aunt, Hattie Granger. Anna says she thinks Miss Martha Morse will give medals to her and Mary Daggett for being the most meddlesome girls in school, judging from the number of times she has spoken to them to-day. Anna is getting to be a regular punster, although I told her that Blair's Rhetoric says that punning is not the highest kind of wit. Mr. Morse met us coming from school in the rain and said it would not hurt us as we were neither sugar nor salt. Anna said, "No, but we are 'lasses." Grandmother has been giving us sulphur and molasses for the purification of the blood and we have to take it three mornings and then skip three mornings. This morning Anna commenced going through some sort of gymnastics and Grandmother asked her what she was doing, and she said it was her first morning to skip.

Abbie Clark had a large tea-party this afternoon and evening—Seminary girls and a few Academy boys. We had a fine supper and then played games. Abbie gave us one which is a test of memory and we tried to learn it from her but she was the only one who could complete it. I can write it down, but not say it:

A good fat hen.

Two ducks and a good fat hen.

Three plump partridges, two ducks and a good fat hen.

Four squawking wild geese, three plump partridges, etc.

Five hundred Limerick oysters.

Six pairs of Don Alfonso's tweezers.

Seven hundred rank and file Macedonian horsemen drawn up in line of battle.

Eight cages of heliogabalus sparrow kites.

Nine sympathetical, epithetical, categorical propositions.

Ten tentapherical tubes.

Eleven flat bottom fly boats sailing between Madagascar and Mount Palermo.

Twelve European dancing masters, sent to teach the Egyptian mummies how to dance, against Hercules' wedding day.

Abbie says it was easier to learn than the multiplication table. They wanted some of us to recite and Abbie Clark gave us Lowell's poem, " John P. Robinson, he, says the world'll go right if he only says Gee! " I gave another of Lowell's poems, " The Courtin'." Julia Phelps had her guitar with her by request and played and sang for us very sweetly. Fred Harrington went home with her and Theodore Barnum with me.

Sunday.—Frankie Richardson asked me to go with her to teach a class in the colored Sunday School on Chapel Street this afternoon. I asked Grandmother if I could go and she said she never noticed that I was particularly interested in the colored race and she said she thought I only wanted an excuse to get out for a walk Sunday afternoon. However, she said I could go just this once. When we got up as far as the Academy, Mr. Noah T. Clarke's brother, who is one of the teachers, came out and Frank said he led the singing at the Sunday School and she said she would give me an introduction to him, so he walked up with us and home again. Grandmother said that when she saw him opening the gate for me, she understood my zeal in missionary work. " The dear little lady," as we often call her, has always been noted for her keen

discernment and wonderful sagacity and loses none
of it as she advances in years. Some one asked
Anna the other day if her Grandmother retained
all her faculties and Anna said, " Yes, indeed, to an
alarming degree." Grandmother knows that we
think she is a perfect angel even if she does seem
rather strict sometimes. Whether we are 7 or
17 we are children to her just the same, and the
Bible says, " Children obey your parents in the
Lord for this is right." We are glad that we never
will seem old to her. I had the same company home
from church in the evening. His home is in
Naples.

Monday.—This morning the cook went to early
mass and Anna told Grandmother she would bake
the pancakes for breakfast if she would let her put
on gloves. She would not let her, so Hannah baked
the cakes. I was invited to Mary Paul's to supper
to-night and drank the first cup of tea I ever drank
in my life. I had a very nice time and Johnnie Paul
came home with me.

Imogen Power and I went down together Friday
afternoon to buy me a Meteorology. We are studying that and Watts on the Mind, instead of
Philosophy.

Tuesday.—I went with Fanny Gaylord to see
Mrs. Callister at the hotel to-night. She is so in-

The Old Canandaigua Academy

terested in all that we tell her, just like " one of the girls."

I was laughing to-day when I came in from the street and Grandmother asked me what amused me so. I told her that I met Mr. and Mrs. Putnam on the street and she looked so immense and he so minute I couldn't help laughing at the contrast. Grandmother said that size was not everything, and then she quoted Cowper's verse:

" Were I so tall to reach the skies or grasp the ocean in a span,
  I must be measured by my soul, the mind is the stature of the man."

I don't believe that helps Mr. Putnam out.

Friday.—We went to Monthly Concert of prayer for Foreign Missions this evening. I told Grandmother that I thought it was not very interesting. Judge Taylor read the *Missionary Herald* about the Madagascans and the Senegambians and the Terra del Fuegans and then Deacon Tyler prayed and they sang " From Greenland's Icy Mountains " and took up a collection and went home. She said she was afraid I did not listen attentively. I don't think I did strain every nerve. I believe Grandmother will give her last cent to Missions if the Boards get into worse straits than they are now.

In Latin class to-day Anna translated the phrase Deo Volente " with violence," and Mr. Tyler, who always enjoys a joke, laughed so, we thought he would fall out of his chair. He evidently thought it was the best one he had heard lately.

November 21.—Aunt Ann gave me a sewing bird to screw on to the table to hold my work instead of pinning it to my knee. Grandmother tells us when we sew or read not to get everything around us that we will want for the next two hours because it is not healthy to sit in one position so long. She wants us to get up and "stir around." Anna does not need this advice as much as I do for she is always on what Miss Achert calls the "qui vive." I am trying to make a sofa pillow out of little pieces of silk. Aunt Ann taught me how. You have to cut pieces of paper into octagonal shape and cover them with silk and then sew them together, over and over. They are beautiful, with bright colors, when they are done. There was a hop at the hotel last night and some of the girls went and had an elegant time. Mr. Hiram Metcalf came here this morning to have Grandmother sign some papers. He always looks very dignified, and Anna and I call him "the deed man." We tried to hear what he said to Grandmother after she signed her name but we only heard something about "fear or compulsion" and Grandmother said "yes." It seems very mysterious. Grandfather took us down street to-day to see the new Star Building. It was the town house and he bought it and got Mr. Warren

Stoddard of Hopewell to superintend cutting it in two and moving the parts separately to Coach Street. When it was completed the shout went up from the crowd, " Hurrah for Thomas Beals, the preserver of the old Court House." No one but Grandfather thought it could be done.

December.—I went with the girls to the lake to skate this afternoon. Mr. Johnson, the colored barber, is the best skater in town. He can skate forwards and backwards and cut all sorts of curlicues, although he is such a heavy man. He is going to Liberia and there his skates won't do him any good. I wish he would give them to me and also his skill to use them. Some one asked me to sit down after I got home and I said I preferred to stand, as I had been sitting down all the afternoon! Gus Coleman took a load of us sleighriding this evening. Of course he had Clara Willson sit on the front seat with him and help him drive.

Thursday.—We had a special meeting of our society this evening at Mary Wheeler's and invited the gentlemen and had charades and general good time. Mr. Gillette and Horace Finley made a great deal of fun for us. We initiated Mr. Gillette into the Dorcas Society, which consists in seating the candidate in a chair and propounding some very solemn questions and then in token of desire to join the society, you ask him to open his mouth very wide

for a piece of cake which you swallow, yourself,
instead! Very disappointing to the new member!
We went to a concert at the Seminary this evening. Miss Mollie Bull sang " Coming Through the
Rye " and Miss Lizzie Bull sang " Annie Laurie "
and "Auld Lang Syne." Jennie Lind, herself,
could not have done better.

December 15.—Alice Jewett, Emma Wheeler and
Anna are in Mrs. Worthington's Sunday School
class and as they have recently united with the
church, she thought they should begin practical
Christian work by distributing tracts among the
neglected classes. So this afternoon they ran away
from school to begin the good work. It was so
bright and pleasant, they thought a walk to the lake
would be enjoyable and they could find a welcome in
some humble home. The girls wanted Anna to be
the leader, but she would only promise that if something pious came into her mind, she would say it.
They knocked at a door and were met by a smiling
mother of twelve children and asked to come in.
They sat down feeling somewhat embarrassed, but
spying a photograph album on the table, they became much interested, while the children explained
the pictures. Finally Anna felt that it was time
to do something, so when no one was looking, she
slipped under one of the books on the table, three
tracts entitled " Consolation for the Bereaved,"
" Systematic Benevolence " and " The Social Evils

of dancing, card playing and theater-going." Then
they said goodbye to their new friends and started
on. They decided not to do any more pastoral
work until another day, but enjoyed the outing very
much.

Christmas.—We all went to Aunt Mary Carr's
to dinner excepting Grandmother, and in the evening
we went to see some tableaux at Dr. Cook's and Dr.
Chapin's at the asylum. We were very much
pleased with the entertainment. Between the acts
Mr. del Pratt, one of the patients, said every time,
" What next! " which made every one laugh.

Grandfather was requested to add his picture to
the gallery of portraits of eminent men for the
Court Room, so he has had it painted. An artist
by the name of Green, who lives in town, has finished it after numerous sittings and brought it up
for our approval. We like it but we do not think
it is as good looking as he is. No one could really
satisfy us probably, so we may as well try to be
suited.

I asked Grandmother if Mr. Clarke could take
Sunday night supper with us and she said she was
afraid he did not know the catechism. I asked him
Friday night and he said he would learn it on Saturday so that he could answer every third question any
way. So he did and got along very well. I think
he deserved a pretty good supper.

1861

March 4, 1861.—President Lincoln was inaugurated to-day.

March 5.—I read the inaugural address aloud to Grandfather this evening. He dwelt with such pathos upon the duty that all, both North and South, owe to the Union, it does not seem as though there could be war!

April.—We seem to have come to a sad, sad time. The Bible says, "A man's worst foes are those of his own household." The whole United States has been like one great household for many years. "United we stand, divided we fall!" has been our watchword, but some who should have been its best friends have proven false and broken the bond. Men are taking sides, some for the North, some for the South. Hot words and fierce looks have followed, and there has been a storm in the air for a long time.

April 15.—The storm has broken upon us. The Confederates fired on Fort Sumter, just off the coast of South Carolina, and forced her on April 14 to haul down the flag and surrender. President

Lincoln has issued a call for 75,000 men and many
are volunteering to go all around us. How strange
and awful it seems.

May, 1861.—Many of the young men are going
from Canandaigua and all the neighboring towns.
It seems very patriotic and grand when they are
singing, " It is sweet, Oh, 'tis sweet, for one's country to die," and we hear the martial music and see
the flags flying and see the recruiting tents on the
square and meet men in uniform at every turn and
see train loads of the boys in blue going to the front,
but it will not seem so grand if we hear they are dead
on the battlefield, far from home. A lot of us girls
went down to the train and took flowers to the soldiers as they were passing through and they cut
buttons from their coats and gave to us as souvenirs.
We have flags on our paper and envelopes, and have
all our stationery bordered with red, white and blue.
We wear little flag pins for badges and tie our hair
with red, white and blue ribbon and have pins and
earrings made of the buttons the soldiers gave us.
We are going to sew for them in our society and
get the garments all cut from the older ladies'
society. They work every day in one of the rooms
of the court house and cut out garments and make
them and scrape lint and roll up bandages. They
say they will provide us with all the garments we
will make. We are going to write notes and enclose
them in the garments to cheer up the soldier boys.

It does not seem now as though I could give up any one who belonged to me. The girls in our society say that if any of the members do send a soldier to the war they shall have a flag bed quilt, made by the society, and have the girls' names on the stars.

May 20.—I recited " Scott and the Veteran " to-day at school, and Mary Field recited, " To Drum Beat and Heart Beat a Soldier Marches By "; Anna recited " The Virginia Mother." Every one learns war poems now-a-days. There was a patriotic rally in Bemis Hall last night and a quartette sang, " The Sword of Bunker Hill " and " Dixie " and " John Brown's Body Lies a Mouldering in the Grave," and many other patriotic songs. We have one West Point cadet, Albert M. Murray, who is in the thick of the fight, and Charles S. Coy represents Canandaigua in the navy.

June, 1861.—At the anniversary exercises, Rev. Samuel M. Hopkins of Auburn gave the address. I have graduated from Ontario Female Seminary after a five years course and had the honor of receiving a diploma from the courtly hands of General John A. Granger. I am going to have it framed and handed down to my grandchildren as a memento, not exactly of sleepless nights and midnight vigils, but of rising betimes, at what Anna calls the crack of dawn. She likes that expression better than daybreak. I heard her reciting in the

The Ontario Female Seminary

back chamber one morning about 4 o'clock and listened at the door. She was saying in the most nonchalant manner: "Science and literature in England were fast losing all traces of originality, invention was discouraged, research unvalued and the examination of nature proscribed. It seemed to be generally supposed that the treasure accumulated in the preceding ages was quite sufficient for all national purposes and that the only duty which authors had to perform was to reproduce what had thus been accumulated, adorned with all the graces of polished style. Tameness and monotony naturally result from a slavish adherence to all arbitrary rules and every branch of literature felt this blighting influence. History, perhaps, was in some degree an exception, for Hume, Robertson and more especially Gibbon, exhibited a spirit of original investigation which found no parallel among their contemporaries." I looked in and asked her where her book was, and she said she left it down stairs. She has "got it" all right, I am sure. We helped decorate the seminary chapel for two days. Our motto was, "Still achieving, still pursuing." Miss Guernsey made most of the letters and Mr. Chubbuck put them up and he hung all the paintings. It was a very warm week. General Granger had to use his palm leaf fan all the time, as well as the rest of us. There were six in our class, Mary Field, Lucy Petherick, Kate Lilly, Sarah Clay, Abby Scott and myself. Abbie Clark would have been in the

class, but she went to Pittsfield, Mass., instead.
General Granger said to each one of us, " It gives me
great pleasure to present you with this diploma,"
and when he gave Miss Scott hers, as she is from
Alabama, he said he wished it might be as a flag of
truce between the North and the South, and this
sentiment was loudly cheered. General Granger
looked so handsome with his black dress suit and
ruffled shirt front and all the natural grace which
belongs to him. The sheepskin has a picture of the
Seminary on it and this inscription: " The Trustees and Faculty of the Ontario Female Seminary
hereby certify that ————— has completed the
course of study prescribed in this Institution, maintained the requisite scholarship and commendable
deportment and is therefore admitted to the gradu-
ating honors of this Institution. President of
Board, John A. Granger; Benjamin F. Richards,
Edward G. Tyler, Principals." Mr. Morse wrote
something for the paper:

" To the Editor of the Repository:
" DEAR SIR—June roses, etc., make our loveliest of
villages a paradise this week. The constellations are
all glorious and the stars of earth far outshine those
of the heavens. The lake shore, ' Lovers' Lane,'
' Glen Kitty ' and the ' Points ' are full of romance and
romancers. The yellow moon and the blue waters
and the dark green shores and the petrified Indians,
whispering stony words at the foot of Genundewah,
and Squaw Island sitting on the waves, like an en-

chanted grove, and 'Whalesback' all humped up in
the East and 'Devil's Lookout' rising over all, made
the 'Sleeping Beauty' a silver sea of witchery and
love; and in the cottages and palaces we ate the
ambrosia and drank the nectar of the sweet goddesses
of this new and golden age.

"I may as well say to you, Mr. Editor, that the
Ontario Female Seminary closed yesterday and
'Yours truly' was present at the commencement. Being a bachelor I shall plead guilty and appeal to the
mercy of the Court, if indicted for undue prejudice
in favor of the charming young orators. After the
report of the Examining Committee, in which the
scholarship of the young ladies was not too highly
praised, came the Latin Salutatory by Miss Clay, a
most beautiful and elegant production (that sentence,
sir, applies to both salutatory and salutatorian). The
'Shadows We Cast,' by Miss Field, carried us far into
the beautiful fields of nature and art and we saw
the dark, or the brilliant shades, which our lives will
cast, upon society and history. Then 'Tongues in
Trees' began to whisper most bewitchingly, and
'Books in the Running Brooks' were opened, and
'Sermons in Stones' were preached by Miss Richards,
and this old bachelor thought if all trees would talk
so well, and every brook would babble so musically,
and each precious stone would exhort so brilliantly,
as they were made to do by the. 'enchantress,' angels
and dreams would henceforth be of little consequence;
and whether the orator should be called 'Tree of
Beauty,' 'Minnehaha' or the 'Kohinoor' is a 'vexata
questio.'

"In the evening Mr. Hardick, 'our own,' whose
hand never touches the piano without making
delicious music, and Misses Daggett and Wilson, also

'our own,' and the musical pupils of the Institution, gave a concert. 'The Young Volunteer' was imperatively demanded, and this for the third time during the anniversary exercises, and was sung amid thunders of applause, 'Star of the South,' Miss Stella Scott, shining meanwhile in all her radiant beauty. May her glorious light soon rest on a Union that shall never more be broken.—Soberly yours,

A Very Old Bachelor."

June, 1861.—There was a patriotic rally this afternoon on the campus of Canandaigua Academy and we Seminary girls went. They raised a flag on the Academy building. General Granger presided, Dr. Coleman led the choir and they sang "The Star Spangled Banner." Mr. Noah T. Clarke made a stirring speech and Mr. Gideon Granger, James C. Smith and E. M. Morse followed. Canandaigua has already raised over $7,000 for the war. Capt. Barry drills the Academy boys in military tactics on the campus every day. Men are constantly enlisting. Lester P. Thompson, son of "Father Thompson," among the others.

A young man asked Anna to take a drive to-day, but Grandmother was not willing at first to let her go. She finally gave her consent, after Anna's plea that he was so young and his horse was so gentle. Just as they were ready to start, I heard Anna run upstairs and I heard him say, "What an Anna!" I asked her afterwards what she went for and she

said she remembered that she had left the soap in
the water.

June.—Dr. Daggett's war sermon from the 146th
Psalm was wonderful.

December 1.—Dr. Carr is dead.   He had a stroke
of paralysis two weeks ago and for several days he
has been unconscious.   The choir of our church,
of which he was leader for so long, and some of the
young people came and stood around his bed and
sang, " Jesus, Lover of My Soul."   They did not
know whether he was conscious or not, but they
thought so because the tears ran down his cheeks
from his closed eyelids, though he could not speak
or move.   The funeral was from the church and
Dr. Daggett's text was, " The Beloved Physician."

1862

January 26.—We went to the Baptist Church this evening to hear Rev. A. H. Lung preach his last sermon before going into the army.

February 17.—Glorious news from the war today. Fort Donelson is taken with 1,500 rebels. The right and the North will surely triumph!

February 21.—Our society met at Fanny Palmer's this afternoon. I went but did not stay to tea as we were going to Madame Anna Bishop's concert in the evening. The concert was very, very good. Her voice has great scope and she was dressed in the latest stage costume, but it took so much material for her skirt that there was hardly any left for the waist.

Washington's Birthday.—Patriotic services were held in the Congregational Church this morning. Madame Anna Bishop sang, and National songs were sung. Hon. James C. Smith read Washington's Farewell Address. In the afternoon a party of twenty-two, young and old, took a ride in the Seminary boat and went to Mr. Paton's on the lake shore road. We carried flags and made it a patri-

"Old Friend Burling"

Madame Anna Bishop

otic occasion. I sat next to Spencer F. Lincoln,
a young man from Naples who is studying law in
Mr. Henry Chesebro's office. I never met him before but he told me he had made up his mind to
go to the war. It is wonderful that young men
who have brilliant prospects before them at home,
will offer themselves upon the altar of their country. I have some new patriotic stationery. There
is a picture of the flag on the envelope and underneath, "If any one attempts to haul down the
American flag shoot him on the spot.—JOHN A.
DIX."

Sunday, February 23.—Everybody came out to
church this morning, expecting to hear Madame
Anna Bishop sing. She was not there, and an
"agent" made a "statement." The audience did
not appear particularly edified.

March 4.—John B. Gough lectured in Bemis Hall
last night and was entertained by Governor Clark.
I told Grandfather that I had an invitation to the
lecture and he asked me who from. I told him
from Mr. Noah T. Clarke's brother. He did not
make the least objection and I was awfully glad,
because he has asked me to the whole course. Wen-
dell Phillips and Horace Greeley, E. H. Chapin and
John G. Saxe and Bayard Taylor are expected.
John B. Gough's lecture was fine. He can make

an audience laugh as much by wagging his coat tails as some men can by talking an hour.

March 26.—I have been up at Laura Chapin's from 10 o'clock in the morning until 10 at night, finishing Jennie Howell's bed quilt, as she is to be married very soon. Almost all of the girls were there. We finished it at 8 p. m. and when we took it off the frames we gave three cheers. Some of the youth of the village came up to inspect our handiwork and see us home. Before we went Julia Phelps sang and played on the guitar and Captain Barry also sang and we all sang together, " O! Columbia, the gem of the ocean, three cheers for the red, white and blue."

June 19.—Our cousin, Ann Eliza Field, was married to-day to George B. Bates at her home on Gibson Street. We went and had an elegant time. Charlie Wheeler made great fun and threw the final shower of rice as they drove away.

June.—There was great excitement in prayer meeting last night, it seemed to Abbie Clark, Mary Field and me on the back seat where we always sit. Several people have asked us why we sit away back there by old Mrs. Kinney, but we tell them that she sits on the other side of the stove from us and we like the seat, because we have occupied it so long. I presume we would see less and hear more if we sat in front. To-night just after Mr. Walter Hubbell had made one of his most beautiful prayers and Mr. Cyrus Dixon was praying, a big June bug came zipping into the room and snapped against the wall and the lights and barely escaped several bald heads. Anna kept dodging around in a most startling manner and I expected every moment to see her walk out and take Emma Wheeler with her, for if she is afraid of anything more than dogs it is June bugs. At this crisis the bug flew out and a cat stealthily walked in. We knew that dear Mrs. Taylor was always unpleasantly affected by the sight of cats and we didn't know what would happen if the cat should go near her. The cat very innocently ascended the steps to the desk and as Judge and Mrs. Taylor always sit on the front seat, she couldn't help observing the ambitious animal as it started to assist Dr. Daggett in conducting the meeting. The result was that Mrs. Taylor just managed to reach the outside door before fainting away. We were glad when the benediction was pronounced.

June.—Anna and I had a serenade last night from the Academy Glee Club, I think, as their voices sounded familiar. We were awakened by the music, about 11 P. M., quite suddenly and I thought I would step across the hall to the front chamber for a match to light the candle. I was only half awake, however, and lost my bearings and stepped off the stairs and rolled or slid to the bottom. The stairs are winding, so I must have performed two or three revolutions before I reached my destination. I jumped up and ran back and found Anna sitting up in bed, laughing. She asked me where I had been and said if I had only told her where I was going she would have gone for me. We decided not to strike a light, but just listen to the singing. Anna said she was glad that the leading tenor did not know how quickly I "tumbled" to the words of his song, "O come my love and be my own, nor longer let me dwell alone," for she thought he would be too much flattered. Grandfather came into the hall and asked if any bones were broken and if he should send for a doctor. We told him we guessed not, we thought we would be all right in the morning. He thought it was Anna who fell down stairs, as he is never looking for such exploits in me. We girls received some verses from the Academy boys, written by Greig Mulligan, under the assumed name of Simon Snooks. The subject was, "The Poor Unfortunate Academy Boys." We have answered them and now I fear Mrs. Grundy will see them and imagine something serious is going on. But she is mistaken and will find, at the end of the session, our hearts are still in our own possession.

When we were down at Sucker Brook the other afternoon we were watching the water and one of the girls said, "How nice it would be if our lives could run along as smoothly as this stream." I said I thought it would be too monotonous. Laura

Chapin said she supposed I would rather have an "eddy" in mine.

We went to the examination at the Academy today and to the gymnasium exercises afterwards. Mr. Noah T. Clarke's brother leads them and they do some great feats with their rings and swings and weights and ladders. We girls can do a few in the bowling alley at the Seminary.

June.—I visited Eureka Lawrence in Syracuse and we attended commencement at Hamilton College, Clinton, and saw there, James Tunnicliff and Stewart Ellsworth of Penn Yan. I also saw Darius Sackett there among the students and also became acquainted with a very interesting young man from Syracuse, with the classic name of Horace Publius Virgilius Bogue. Both of these young men are studying for the ministry. I also saw Henry P. Cook, who used to be one of the Academy boys, and Morris Brown, of Penn Yan. They talk of leaving college and going to the war and so does Darius Sackett.

July, 1862.—The President has called for 300,000 more brave men to fill up the ranks of the fallen. We hear every day of more friends and acquaintances who have volunteered to go.

August 20.—The 126th Regiment, just organized, was mustered into service at Camp Swift, Geneva.

Those that I know who belong to it are Colonel
E. S. Sherrill, Lieutenant Colonel James M. Bull,
Captain Charles A. Richardson, Captain Charles M.
Wheeler, Captain Ten Eyck Munson, Captain Orin
G. Herendeen, Surgeon Dr. Charles S. Hoyt, Hos-
pital Steward Henry T. Antes, First Lieutenant
Charles Gage, Second Lieutenant Spencer F. Lin-
coln, First Sergeant Morris Brown, Corporal Hol-
lister N. Grimes, Privates Darius Sackett, Henry
Willson, Oliver Castle, William Lamport.

Dr. Hoyt wrote home: "God bless the dear
ones we leave behind; and while you try to perform
the duties you owe to each other, we will try to
perform ours."

We saw by the papers that the volunteers of the
regiment before leaving camp at Geneva allotted
over $15,000 of their monthly pay to their families
and friends at home.   One soldier sent this telegram
to his wife, as the regiment started for the front:
"God bless you. Hail Columbia. Kiss the baby.
Write soon." A volume in ten words.

August.—The New York State S. S. convention
is convened here and the meetings are most interesting. They were held in our church and lasted three
days. A Mr. Hart, from New York, led the singing and Mr. Ralph Wells was Moderator. Mr.
Noah T. Clarke was in his element all through the
meetings. Mr. Pardee gave some fine blackboard
exercises. During the last afternoon Mr. Tousley

was wheeled into the church, in his invalid chair, and said a few words, which thrilled every one. So much tenderness, mingled with his old time enthusiasm and love for the cause. It is the last time probably that his voice will ever be heard in public. They closed the grand meeting with the hymn beginning:

> " Blest be the tie that binds
> Our hearts in Christian love."

In returning thanks to the people of Canandaigua for their generous entertainment, Mr. Ralph Wells facetiously said that the cost of the convention must mean something to Canandaigua people, for the cook in one home was heard to say, " These religiouses do eat awful! "

September 13.—Darius Sackett was wounded by a musket shot in the leg, at Maryland Heights, Va., and in consequence is discharged from the service.

September.—Edgar A. Griswold of Naples is recruiting a company here for the 148th Regiment, of which he is captain. Hiram P. Brown, Henry S. Murray and Charles H. Paddock are officers in the company. Dr. Elnathan W. Simmons is surgeon.

September 22.—I read aloud to Grandfather this evening the Emancipation Proclamation issued as

a war measure by President Lincoln, to take effect
January 1, liberating over three million slaves. He
recommends to all thus set free, to labor faithfully
for reasonable wages and to abstain from all violence, unless in necessary self-defense, and he in-
vokes upon this act "the considerate judgment of
mankind and the gracious favor of Almighty God."

November 21.—This is my twentieth birthday.
Anna wanted to write a poem for the occasion and
this morning she handed me what she called "An
effort." She said she wrestled with it all night long
and could not sleep and this was the result:

> "One hundred years from now, Carrie dear,
> In all probability you'll not be here;
> But we'll all be in the same boat, too,
> And there'll be no one left
> To say boo hoo!"

Grandfather gave me for a present a set of books
called "Irving's Catechisms on Ancient Greeks and
Romans." They are four little books bound in
leather, which were presented to our mother for a
prize. It is thus inscribed on the front page, "Miss
Elizabeth Beals at a public examination of the Female Boarding School in East Bloomfield, October
15, 1825, was judged to excel the school in Reading.
In testimony of which she receives this Premium
from her affectionate instructress, S. Adams."
I cannot imagine Grandmother sending us away

to boarding school, but I suppose she had so many children then, she could spare one or two as well as not. She says they sent Aunt Ann to Miss Willard's school at Troy. I received a birthday letter from Mrs. Beaumont to-day. She wants to know how everything goes at the Seminary and if Anna still occupies the front seat in the school room most of the time. She says she supposes she is quite a sedate young lady now but she hopes there is a whole lot of the old Anna left. I think there is.

December.—Hon. William H. Lamport went down to Virginia to see his son and found that he had just died in the hospital from measles and pneumonia. Their only son, only eighteen years old!

1863

January.—Grandmother went to Aunt Mary Carr's to tea to-night, very much to our surprise, for she seldom goes anywhere. Anna said she was going to keep house exactly as Grandmother did, so after supper she took a little hot water in a basin on a tray and got the tea-towels and washed the silver and best china but she let the ivory handles on the knives and forks get wet, so I presume they will all turn black. Grandmother never lets her little nice things go out into the kitchen, so probably that is the reason that everything is forty years old and yet as good as new. She let us have the Young Ladies' Aid Society here to supper because I am President. She came into the parlor and looked at our basket of work, which the older ladies cut out for us to make for the soldiers. She had the supper table set the whole length of the dining room and let us preside at the table. Anna made the girls laugh so, they could hardly eat, although they said everything was splendid. They said they never ate better biscuit, preserves, or fruit cake and the coffee was delicious. After it was over, the " dear little lady " said she hoped we had a good time. After the girls were gone Grandmother wanted to look over the garments and see how much we had accom-

plished and if we had made them well.   Mary Field
made a pair of drawers with No. 90 thread.   She
said she wanted them to look fine and I am sure
they did.   Most of us wrote notes and put inside
the garments for the soldiers in the hospitals.

Sarah Gibson Howell has had an answer to her
letter.   His name is Foster—a Major.   She ex-
pects him to come and see her soon.

All the girls wear newspaper bustles to school
now and Anna's rattled to-day and Emma Wheeler
heard it and said, "What's the news, Anna?"
They both laughed out loud and found that "the
latest news from the front" was that Miss Morse
kept them both after school and they had to copy
Dictionary for an hour.   War prices are terrible.
I paid $3.50 to-day for a hoop skirt.

January 13.—P. T. Barnum delivered his lecture
on "The Art of Money Getting" in Bemis Hall this
evening for the benefit of the Ladies' Aid Society,
which is working for the soldiers.   We girls went
and enjoyed it.

February.—The members of our society sympa-
thized with General McClellan when he was criti-
cised by some and we wrote him the following letter:

"CANANDAIGUA, *Feb.* 13, 1863.
"MAJ. GEN. GEO. McCLELLAN:
"Will you pardon any seeming impropriety in our
addressing you, and attribute it to the impulsive love

and admiration of hearts which see in you, the bravest
and noblest defender of our Union. We cannot resist
the impulse to tell you, be our words ever so feeble,
how our love and trust have followed you from Rich
Mountain to Antietam, through all slanderous attacks
of traitorous politicians and fanatical defamers—how
we have admired, not less than your calm courage on
the battlefield, your lofty scorn of those who remained
at home in the base endeavor to strip from your brow
the hard earned laurels placed there by a grateful
country: to tell further, that in your forced retirement
from battlefields of the Republic's peril, you have ' but
changed your country's arms for more,—your country's heart,'—and to assure you that so long as our
country remains to us a sacred name and our flag
a holy emblem, so long shall we cherish your memory
as the defender and protector of both. We are an
association whose object it is to aid, in the only way
in which woman, alas! can aid our brothers in the
field. Our sympathies are with them in the cause
for which they have periled all—our hearts are
with them in the prayer, that ere long their beloved
commander may be restored to them, and that once
more as of old he may lead them to victory in the
sacred name of the Union and Constitution.

"With united prayers that the Father of all may
have you and yours ever in His holy keeping, we
remain your devoted partisans."

Signed by a large number.

The following in reply was addressed to the lady
whose name was first signed to the above:

"New York, *Feb.* 21, 1863.

"Madam—I take great pleasure in acknowledging
the receipt of the very kind letter of the 13th inst.,

from yourself and your friends. Will you do me the favor to say to them how much I thank them for it, and that I am at a loss to express my gratitude for the pleasant and cheering terms in which it is couched. Such sentiments on the part of those whose brothers have served with me in the field are more grateful to me than anything else can be. I feel far more than rewarded by them for all I have tried to accomplish. —I am, Madam, with the most sincere respect and friendship, yours very truly,

" Geo. B. McClellan."

May.—A number of the teachers and pupils of the Academy have enlisted for the war. Among them E. C. Clarke, H. C. Kirk, A. T. Wilder, Norman K. Martin, T. C. Parkhurst, Mr. Gates. They have a tent on the square and are enlisting men in Canandaigua and vicinity for the 4th N. Y. Heavy Artillery. I received a letter from Mr. Noah T. Clarke's mother in Naples. She had already sent three sons, Bela, William and Joseph, to the war and she is very sad because her youngest has now enlisted. She says she feels as did Jacob of old when he said, " I am bereaved of my children. Joseph is not and Simeon is not and now you will take Benjamin away." I have heard that she is a beautiful singer but she says she cannot sing any more until this cruel war is over. I wish that I could write something to comfort her but I feel as Mrs. Browning puts it : " If you want a song for your Italy free, let none look at me."

Our society met at Fannie Pierce's this afternoon. Her mother is an invalid and never gets out at all, but she is very much interested in the soldiers and in all young people, and loves to have us come in and see her and we love to go.   She enters into the plans of all of us young girls and has a personal interest in us.   We had a very good time to-night and Laura Chapin was more full of fun than usual. Once there was silence for a minute or two and some one said, " awful pause." Laura said, " I guess you would have awful paws if you worked as hard as I do."   We were talking about how many of us girls would be entitled to flag bed quilts, and according to the rules, they said that, up to date, Abbie Clark and I were the only ones.   The explanation is that Captain George N. Williams and Lieutenant E. C. Clarke are enlisted in their country's service. Susie Daggett is Secretary and Treasurer of the Society and she reported that in one year's time we made in our society 133 pairs of drawers, 101 shirts, 4 pairs socks for soldiers, and 54 garments for the families of soldiers.

Abbie Clark and I had our ambrotypes taken to-day for two young braves who are going to the war. William H. Adams is also commissioned Captain and is going to the front.

July 4.—The terrible battle of Gettysburg brings to Canandaigua sad news of our soldier boys of the 126th Regiment.   Colonel Sherrill was instantly

"Abbie Clark   and I
had our ambrotypes taken to-day"

"Mr. Noah T. Clarke's
Brother and I"

killed, also Captains Wheeler and Herendeen, Henry Willson and Henry P. Cook. Captain Richardson was wounded.

July 26.—Charlie Wheeler was buried with military honors from the Congregational church to-day. Two companies of the 54th New York State National Guard attended the funeral, and the church was packed, galleries and all. It was the saddest funeral and the only one of a soldier that I ever attended. I hope it will be the last. He was killed at Gettysburg, July 3, by a sharpshooter's bullet. He was a very bright young man, graduate of Yale college and was practising law. He was captain of Company K, 126th N. Y. Volunteers. I have copied an extract from Mr. Morse's lecture, " You and I ": " And who has forgotten that gifted youth, who fell on the memorable field of Gettysburg? To win a noble name, to save a beloved country, he took his place beneath the dear old flag, and while cannon thundered and sabers clashed and the stars of the old Union shone above his head he went down in the shock of battle and left us desolate, a name to love and a glory to endure. And as we solemnly know, as by the old charter of liberty we most sacredly swear, he was truly and faithfully and religiously

> Of all our friends the noblest,
> The choicest and the purest,
> The nearest and the dearest,
>   In the field at Gettysburg.

Of all the heroes bravest,
Of soul the brightest, whitest,
Of all the warriors greatest,
    Shot dead at Gettysburg.

And where the fight was thickest,
And where the smoke was blackest,
And where the fire was hottest,
    On the fields of Gettysburg,
There flashed his steel the brightest,
There blazed his eyes the fiercest,
There flowed his blood the reddest
    On the field of Gettysburg.

O wailing winds of heaven!
O weeping dew of evening!
O music of the waters
    That flow at Gettysburg,
Mourn tenderly the hero,
The rare and glorious hero,
The loved and peerless hero,
    Who died at Gettysburg.

His turf shall be the greenest,
His roses bloom the sweetest,
His willow droop the saddest
    Of all at Gettysburg.
His memory live the freshest,
His fame be cherished longest,
Of all the holy warriors,
    Who fell at Gettysburg.

These were patriots, these were our jewels.
When shall we see their like again? And of every
soldier who has fallen in this war his friends may

write just as lovingly as you and I may do of those
to whom I pay my feeble tribute."

August, 1863.—The U. S. Sanitary Commission
has been organized. Canandaigua sent Dr. W. Fitch
Cheney to Gettysburg with supplies for the sick and
wounded and he took seven assistants with him.
Home bounty was brought to the tents and put into
the hands of the wounded soldiers.   A blessed work.

August 12.—Lucilla Field was married in our
church to-day to Rev. S. W. Pratt. I always
thought she was cut out for a minister's wife.
Jennie Draper cried herself sick because Lucilla,
her Sunday School teacher, is going away.

October 8.—News came to-day of the death of
Lieutenant Hiram Brown. He died of fever at
Portsmouth, only little more than a year after he
went away.

November 1.—The 4th New York Heavy Artillery is stationed at Fort Hamilton, N. Y. harbor.
Uncle Edward has invited me down to New York
to spend a month! Very opportune! Grandfather
says that I can go and Miss Rosewarne is beginning
a new dress for me to-day.

November 6.—We were saddened to-day by news
of the death of Augustus Torrey Wilder in the hospital at Fort Ethan Allen.

November 9.—No. 68 E. 19th Street, New York City. Grandfather and I came from Canandaigua yesterday. He is at Gramercy Park Hotel. We were met by a military escort of " one " at Albany and consequently came through more safely, I suppose. James met us at the station in New York. He lives at Uncle Edward's; attends to all of his legal business and is his confidential clerk. I like it very much here. They are very stylish and grand but I don't mind that. Aunt Emily is reserved and dignified but very kind. People do not pour their tea or coffee into their saucers any more to cool it, but drink it from the cup, and you must mind and not leave your teaspoon in your cup. I notice everything and am very particular. Mr. Morris K. Jesup lives right across the street and I see him every day, as he is a friend of Uncle Edward. Grandfather has gone back home and left me in charge of friends " a la militaire " and others.

November 15.—" We " went out to Fort Hamilton to-day and are going to Blackwell's Island to-morrow and to many other places of interest down the Bay. Soldiers are everywhere and I feel quite important, walking around in company with blue coat and brass buttons—very becoming style of dress for men and the military salute at every turn is what one reads about.

Sunday.—Went to Broadway Tabernacle to church to-day and heard Rev. Joseph P. Thompson

preach. Abbie Clark is visiting her sister, Mrs.
Fred Thompson, and sat a few seats ahead of us in
church. She turned around and saw us. We also
saw Henrietta Francis Talcott, who was a " Seminary girl." She wants me to come to see her in
her New York home.

November 19.—We wish we were at Gettysburg
to-day to hear President Lincoln's and Edward Everett's addresses at the dedication of the National
Cemetery. We will read them in to-morrow's papers, but it will not be like hearing them.

Author's Note, 1911.—Forty-eight years have
elapsed since Lincoln's speech was delivered at the
dedication of the Soldiers' Cemetery at Gettysburg.
So eloquent and remarkable was his utterance that I
believe I am correct in stating that every word
spoken has now been translated into all known lan-
guages and is regarded as one of the World Classics.
The same may be said of Lincoln's letter to the
mother of five sons lost in battle. I make no apology
for inserting in this place both the speech and the
letter. Mr. Whitelaw Reid, the American Ambas-
sador to Great Britain, in an address on Lincoln delivered at the University of Birmingham in December, 1910, remarked in reference to this letter,
" What classic author in our common English
tongue has surpassed that?" and next may I ask,
" What English or American orator has on a similar

occasion surpassed this address on the battlefield of Gettysburg?"

"Four score and seven years ago, our fathers brought forth on this continent a new nation conceived in liberty and dedicated to the proposition that all men are created equal. Now we are engaged in a great civil war, testing whether that nation, or any nation so conceived and so dedicated, can long endure. We are met on a great battlefield of that war. We have come to dedicate a portion of that field as a final resting place for those who gave their lives that that nation might live. It is altogether fitting and proper that we should do this. But in a larger sense we cannot dedicate—we cannot consecrate—we cannot hallow this ground. The brave men, living and dead, who struggled here have consecrated it far above our poor power to add or detract. The world will little note, nor long remember, what we say here—but it can never forget what they did here. It is for us, the living, rather, to be dedicated here to the unfinished work which they who fought here have thus far so nobly advanced. It is rather for us to be here dedicated to the great task remaining before us—that from these honored dead we take increased devotion to that cause for which they gave the last full measure of devotion—that we here highly resolve, that these dead shall not have died in vain—that this nation under God shall have a new birth of freedom—and that government of the people, by the people and for the people, shall not perish from the earth."

It was during the dark days of the war that he wrote this simple letter of sympathy to a bereaved mother:—

"I have been shown, in the files of the War Department, a statement that you are the mother of five sons who have died gloriously on the field of battle. I feel how weak and fruitless must be any words of mine which should attempt to beguile you from your grief for a loss so overwhelming, but I cannot refrain from tendering to you the consolation which may be found in the thanks of the Republic they died to save. I pray that our Heavenly Father may assuage the anguish of your bereavement, and leave you only the cherished memory of the loved and lost, and the solemn pride that must be yours, to have laid so costly a sacrifice upon the altar of Freedom."

November 21.—Abbie Clark and her cousin Cora came to call and invited me and her soldier cousin to come to dinner to-night, at Mrs. Thompson's. He will be here this afternoon and I will give him the invitation. James is asked for the evening.

November 22.—We had a delightful visit. Mr. Thompson took us up into his den and showed us curios from all over the world and as many pictures as we would find in an art gallery.

Friday.—Last evening Uncle Edward took a party of us, including Abbie Clark, to Wallack's Theater to see "Rosedale," which is having a great run. I enjoyed it and told James it was the best play I ever "heard." He said I must not say that I "heard" a play. I "saw" it. I stand corrected.

I told James that I heard of a young girl who
went abroad and on her return some one asked her
if she saw King Lear and she said, no, he was sick
all the time she was there! I just loved the play
last night and laughed and cried in turn, it seemed
so real. I don't know what Grandmother will say,
but I wrote her about it and said, " When you are
with the Romans, you must do as the Romans do."
I presume she will say " that is not the way you were
brought up."

December 7.—The 4th New York Heavy Artillery has orders to move to Fort Ethan Allen, near
Washington, and I have orders to return to Canandaigua. I have enjoyed the five weeks very much
and as " the soldier " was on parole most of the time
I have seen much of interest in the city. Uncle
Edward says that he has lived here forty years but
has never visited some of the places that we have
seen, so he told me when I mentioned climbing to
the top of Trinity steeple.

CANANDAIGUA, *December* 8.—Home again. I
had military attendance as far as Paterson, N. J.,
and came the rest of the way with strangers. Not
caring to talk I liked it just as well. When I said
good bye I could not help wondering whether it
was for years, or forever. This cruel war is terrible and precious lives are being sacrificed and

hearts broken every day.   What is to be the result?
We can only trust and wait.

Christmas Eve, 1863.—Sarah Gibson Howell was
married to Major Foster this evening.   She invited
all the society and many others.   It was a beautiful
wedding and we all enjoyed it.   Some time ago I
asked her to write in my album and she sewed a
lock of her black curling hair on the page and in the
center of it wrote, " Forget not Gippie."

December 31.—Our brother John was married in
Boston to-day to Laura Arnold, a lovely girl.

1864

April 1.—Grandfather had decided to go to New York to attend the fair given by the Sanitary Commission, and he is taking two immense books, which are more than one hundred years old, to present to the Commission, for the benefit of the war fund.

April 18.—Grandfather returned home to-day, unexpectedly to us. I knew he was sick when I met him at the door. He had traveled all night alone from New York, although he said that a stranger, a fellow passenger, from Ann Arbor, Mich., on the train noticed that he was suffering and was very kind to him. He said he fell in his room at Gramercy Park Hotel in the night, and his knee was very painful. We sent for old Dr. Cheney and he said the hurt was a serious one and needed most careful attention. I was invited to a spelling school at Abbie Clark's in the evening and Grandmother said that she and Anna would take care of Grandfather till I got back, and then I could sit up by him the rest of the night. We spelled down and had quite a merry time. Major C. S. Aldrich had escaped from prison and was there. He came home with me, as my soldier is down in Virginia.

April 19.—Grandfather is much worse. He was
delirious all night. We have sent for Dr. Rosewarne in counsel and Mrs. Lightfoote has come to
stay with us all the time and we have sent for Aunt
Glorianna.

April 20.—Grandfather dictated a letter to-night
to a friend of his in New York. After I had finished he asked me if I had mended his gloves. I
said no, but I would have them ready when he
wanted them. Dear Grandfather! he looks so sick
I fear he will never wear his gloves again.

May 16.—I have not written in my diary for a
month and it has been the saddest month of my life.
Dear, dear Grandfather is dead. He was buried
May 2, just two weeks from the day that he returned
from New York. We did everything for him that
could be done, but at the end of the first week the
doctors saw that he was beyond all human aid.
Uncle Thomas told the doctors that they must tell
him. He was much surprised but received the ver-
dict calmly. He said " he had no notes out and
perhaps it was the best time to go." He had taught
us how to live and he seemed determined to show
us how a Christian should die. He said he wanted
" Grandmother and the children to come to him and
have all the rest remain outside." When we came
into the room he said to Grandmother, " Do you
know what the doctors say? " She bowed her head,

and then he motioned for her to come on one side
and Anna and me on the other and kneel by his bed-
side.   He placed a hand upon us and upon her and
said to her, " All the rest seem very much excited,
but you and I must be composed."   Then he asked
us to say the 23d Psalm, " The Lord is my Shepherd," and then all of us said the Lord's Prayer
together after Grandmother had offered a little
prayer for grace and strength in this trying hour.
Then he said, " Grandmother, you must take care of
the girls, and, girls, you must take care of Grandmother."   We felt as though our hearts would
break and were sure we never could be happy again.
During the next few days he often spoke of dying
and of what we must do when he was gone.   Once
when I was sitting by him he looked up and smiled
and said, " You will lose all your roses watching
over me."   A good many business men came in to
see him to receive his parting blessing.   The two
McKechnie brothers, Alexander and James, came in
together on their way home from church the Sunday
before he died.   Dr. Daggett came very often.   Mr.
Alexander Howell and Mrs. Worthington came, too.

He lived until Saturday, the 30th, and in the
morning he said, " Open the door wide."   We did
so and he said, " Let the King of Glory enter in."
Very soon after he said, " I am going home to
Paradise," and then sank into that sleep which on
this earth knows no waking.   I sat by the window
near his bed and watched the rain beat into the

grass and saw the peonies and crocuses and daffodils beginning to come up out of the ground and I thought to myself, I shall never see the flowers come up again without thinking of these sad, sad days. He was buried Monday afternoon, May 2, from the Congregational church, and Dr. Daggett preached a sermon from a favorite text of Grandfather's, " I shall die in my nest." James and John came and as we stood with dear Grandmother and all the others around his open grave and heard Dr. Daggett say in his beautiful sympathetic voice, " Earth to earth, ashes to ashes, dust to dust," we felt that we were losing our best friend; but he told us that we must live for Grandmother and so we will.

The next Sabbath, Anna and I were called out of church by a messenger, who said that Grandmother was taken suddenly ill and was dying. When we reached the house attendants were all about her administering restoratives, but told us she was rapidly sinking. I asked if I might speak to her and was reluctantly permitted, as they thought best not to disturb her. I sat down by her and with tearful voice said, " Grandmother, don't you know that Grandfather said we were to care for you and you were to care for us and if you die we cannot do as Grandfather said?" She opened her eyes and looked at me and said quietly, " Dry your eyes, child, I shall not die to-day or to-morrow." She seems well now.

Inscribed in my diary:

" They are passing away, they are passing away,
Not only the young, but the aged and gray.
Their places are vacant, no longer we see
The armchair in waiting, as it used to be.
The hat and the coat are removed from the nail,
Where for years they have hung, every day without
    fail.
The shoes and the slippers are needed no more,
Nor kept ready waiting, as they were of yore,
The desk which he stood at in manhood's fresh
    prime,
Which now shows the marks of the finger of time,
The bright well worn keys, which were childhood's
    delight
Unlocking the treasures kept hidden from sight.
These now are mementoes of him who has passed,
Who stands there no longer, as we saw him last.
Other hands turn the keys, as he did, before,
Other eyes will his secrets, if any, explore.
The step once elastic, but feeble of late,
No longer we watch for through doorway or gate,
Though often we turn, half expecting to see,
The loved one approaching, but ah! 'tis not he.
We miss him at all times, at morn when we meet,
For the social repast, there is one vacant seat.
At noon, and at night, at the hour of prayer,
Our hearts fill with sadness, one voice is not there.
Yet not without hope his departure we mourn,
In faith and in trust, all our sorrows are borne,
Borne upward to Him who in kindness and love
Sends earthly afflictions to draw us above.
Thus hoping and trusting, rejoicing, we'll go,
Both upward and onward through weal and through
    woe

'Till all of life's changes and conflicts are past
Beyond the dark river, to meet him at last."

In Memoriam

Thomas Beals died in Canandaigua, N. Y., on Saturday, April 30th, 1864, in the 81st year of his age. Mr. Beals was born in Boston, Mass., November 13, 1783.

He came to this village in October, 1803, only 14 years after the first settlement of the place. He was married in March, 1805, to Abigail Field, sister of the first pastor of the Congregational church here. Her family, in several of its branches, have since been distinguished in the ministry, the legal profession, and in commercial enterprise.

Living to a good old age, and well known as one of our most wealthy and respected citizens, Mr. Beals is another added to the many examples of successful men who, by energy and industry, have made their own fortune.

On coming to this village, he was teacher in the Academy for a time, and afterward entered into mercantile business, in which he had his share of vicissitude. When the Ontario Savings Bank was established, 1832, he became the Treasurer, and managed it successfully till the institution ceased, in 1835, with his withdrawal. In the meantime he conducted, also, a banking business of his own, and this was continued until a week previous to his death, when he formally withdrew, though for the last five years devolving its more active duties upon his son.

As a banker, his sagacity and fidelity won for him the confidence and respect of all classes of persons in this community. The business portion of our village is very much indebted to his enterprise for the eligible structures he built that have more than made good the losses sustained by fires. More than fifty years ago he was actively concerned in the building of the Congregational church, and also superintended the erection of the county jail and almshouse; for many years a trustee of Canandaigua Academy, and trustee and treasurer of the Congregational church. At the time of his death he and his wife, who survives him, were the oldest members of the church, having united with it in 1807, only eight years after its organization. Until hindered by the infirmities of age, he was a constant attendant of its services and ever devoutly maintained the worship of God in his family. No person has been more generally known among all classes of our citizens. Whether at home or abroad he could not fail to be remarked for his gravity and dignity. His character was original, independent, and his manners remarkable for a dignified courtesy. Our citizens were familiar with his brief, emphatic answers with the wave of his hand. He was fond of books, a great reader, collected a valuable number of volumes, and was happy in the use of language both in writing and conversation. In many unusual ways he often showed his kind consideration for the poor and afflicted, and many persons hearing of his death gratefully recollect instances, not known to others, of his seasonable kindness to them in trouble. In his charities he often studied concealment as carefully as others court display. His marked individuality of character and deportment, together with his shrewd discernment and active habits, could not fail to leave a distinct impression on the minds of all.

For more than sixty years he transacted business in one place here, and his long life thus teaches more than one generation the value of sobriety, diligence, fidelity and usefulness.

In his last illness he remarked to a friend that he always loved Canandaigua; had done several things for its prosperity, and had intended to do more. He had known his measure of affliction; only four of eleven children survive him, but children and children's children ministered to the comfort of his last days. Notwithstanding his years and infirmities, he was able to visit New York, returning April 18th quite unwell, but not immediately expecting a fatal termination. As the final event drew near, he seemed happily prepared to meet it. He conversed freely with his friends and neighbors in a softened and benignant spirit, at once receiving and imparting benedictions. His end seemed to realize his favorite citation from Job: "I shall die in my nest."

His funeral was attended on Monday in the Congregational church by a large assembly, Dr. Daggett, the pastor, officiating on the occasion.—Written by Dr. O. E. Daggett in 1864.

May.—The 4th New York Heavy Artillery is having hard times in the Virginia mud and rain. They are near Culpeper. It is such a change from their snug winter quarters at Fort Ethan Allen. There are 2,800 men in the Regiment and 1,200 are sick. Dr. Charles S. Hoyt of the 126th, which is camping close by, has come to the help of these new recruits so kindly as to win every heart, quite in contrast to the heartlessness of their own surgeons. They will always love him for this. It is just like him.

June 22.—Captain Morris Brown, of Penn Yan, was killed to-day by a musket shot in the head, while commanding the regiment before Petersburg.

June 23, 1864.—Anna graduated last Thursday, June 16, and was valedictorian of her class. There were eleven girls in the class, Ritie Tyler, Mary Antes, Jennie Robinson, Hattie Paddock, Lillie Masters, Abbie Hills, Miss McNair, Miss Pardee and Miss Palmer, Miss Jasper and Anna. The subject of her essay was " The Last Time." I will copy an account of the exercises as they appeared

in this week's village paper.   Every one thinks it
was written by Mr. E. M. Morse.

A WORD FROM AN OLD MAN

" Mr. Editor:
  "Less than a century ago I was traveling through
this enchanted region and accidentally heard that it
was commencement week at the seminary. I went.
My venerable appearance seemed to command respect
and I received many attentions.   I presented my snowy
head and patriarchal beard at the doors of the sacred
institution and was admitted.   I heard all the classes,
primary, secondary, tertiary, et cetera.   All went
merry as a marriage bell.   Thursday was the great
day.   I made vast preparation.   I rose early, dressed
with much care.   I affectionately pressed the hands
of my two landlords and left.   When I arrived at
the seminary I saw at a glance that it was a place
where true merit was appreciated.   I was invited to
a seat among the dignitaries, but declined.   I am a
modest man, I always was.   I recognized the benign
Principals of the school.   You can find no better prin-
ciples in the states than in Ontario Female Seminary.
After the report of the committee a very lovely young
lady arose and saluted us in Latin.   I looked very
wise, I always do.   So did everybody.   We all understood it.   As she proceeded, I thought the grand old
Roman tongue had never sounded so musically and
when she pronounced the decree, ' Richmond delenda
est,' we all hoped it might be prophetic.   Then followed the essays of the other young ladies and then
every one waited anxiously for ' The Last Time.'
At last it came.   The story was beautifully told, the
adieux were tenderly spoken.   We saw the withered

flowers of early years scattered along the academic ways, and the golden fruit of scholarly culture ripening in the gardens of the future. Enchanted by the sorrowful eloquence, bewildered by the melancholy brilliancy, I sent a rosebud to the charming valedictorian and wandered out into the grounds. I went to the concert in the evening and was pleased and delighted. So was everybody. I shall return next year unless the gout carries me off. I hope I shall hear just such beautiful music, see just such beautiful faces and dine at the same excellent hotel.

Senex."

Anna closed her valedictory with these words:

"May we meet at one gate when all's over;
    The ways they are many and wide,
And seldom are two ways the same;
    Side by side may we stand
At the same little door when all's done.
    The ways they are many,
    The end it is one."

July 10.—We have had word of the death of Spencer F. Lincoln. One more brave soldier sacrificed.

August.—The New York State S. S. Convention was held in Buffalo and among others Fanny Gaylord, Mary Field and myself attended. We had a fine time and were entertained at the home of Mr. and Mrs. Sexton. Her mother is living with her, a dear old lady who was Judge Atwater's daughter

and used to go to school to Grandfather Beals. We
went with other delegates on an excursion to
Niagara Falls and went into the express office at the
R. R. station to see Grant Schley, who is express
agent there. He said it seemed good to see so many
home faces.

September 1.—My war letters come from George-
town Hospital now. Mr. Noah T. Clarke is very
anxious and sends telegrams to Andrew Chesebro
every day to go and see his brother.

September 30.—To-day the " Benjamin " of the
family reached home under the care of Dr. J. Byron
Hayes, who was sent to Washington after him. I
went over to Mr. Noah T. Clarke's to see him and
found him just a shadow of his former self. However, " hope springs eternal in the human breast "
and he says he knows he will soon be well again.
This is his thirtieth birthday and it is glorious that
he can spend it at home.

October 1.—Mr. Noah T. Clarke accompanied
his brother to-day to the old home in Naples and
found two other soldier brothers, William and Joseph, had just arrived on leave of absence from the
army so the mother's heart sang " Praise God from
whom all blessings flow." The fourth brother has
also returned to his home in Illinois, disabled.

November.—They are holding Union Revival
Services in town now.   One evangelist from out of
town said he would call personally at the homes and
ask if all were Christians.   Anna told Grandmother
if he came here she should tell him about her.
Grandmother said we must each give an account
for ourselves.   Anna said she should tell him about
her little Grandmother anyway.   We saw him coming up the walk about 11 A.M. and Anna went to
the door and asked him in.   They sat down in the
parlor and he remarked about the pleasant weather
and Canandaigua such a beautiful town and the people so cultured.   She said yes, she found the town
every way desirable and the people pleasant, though
she had heard it remarked that strangers found it
hard to get acquainted and that you had to have
a residence above the R. R. track and give a satisfactory answer as to who your Grandfather was,
before admittance was granted to the best society.
He said he had been kindly received everywhere.
She said "everybody likes ministers."   (He was
quite handsome and young.)   He asked her how
long she had lived here and she told him nearly all
of her brief existence!   She said if he had asked
her how old she was she would have told him she
was so young that Will Adams last May was appointed her guardian.   He asked how many there
were in the family and she said her Grandmother,
her sister and herself.   He said, " They are Christians, I suppose."   " Yes," she said, " my sister is a

S. S. teacher and my Grandmother was born a Christian, about 80 years ago." " Indeed," he said. " I would like to see her." Anna said she would have to be excused as she seldom saw company. When he arose to go he said, " My dear young lady, I trust that you are a Christian." " Mercy yes," she said, " years ago." He said he was very glad and hoped she would let her light shine. She said that was what she was always doing—that the other night at a revival meeting she sang every verse of every hymn and came home feeling as though she had herself personally rescued by hand at least fifty " from sin and the grave." He smiled approvingly and bade her good bye. She told Grandmother she presumed he would say " he had not found so great faith, no not in Israel."

We have Teachers' meetings now and Mrs. George Wilson leads and instructs us on the Sunday School lesson for the following Sunday. We met at Mrs. Worthington's this evening. I think Mrs. Wilson knows Barnes' notes, Cruden's Concordance, the Westminster Catechism and the Bible from beginning to end.

1865

March 5.—I have just read President Lincoln's second inaugural address. It only takes five minutes to read it but, oh, how much it contains.

March 20.—Hardly a day passes that we do not hear news of Union victories. Every one predicts that the war is nearly at an end.

March 29.—An officer arrived here from the front yesterday and he said that, on Saturday morning, shortly after the battle commenced which resulted so gloriously for the Union in front of Petersburg, President Lincoln, accompanied by General Grant and staff, started for the battlefield, and reached there in time to witness the close of the contest and the bringing in of the prisoners. His presence was immediately recognized and created the most intense enthusiasm. He afterwards rode over the battlefield, listened to the report of General Parke to General Grant, and added his thanks for the great service rendered in checking the onslaught of the rebels and in capturing so many of their number. I read this morning the order of Secretary Stanton for the flag raising on Fort Sumter. It reads thus: " War department, Adjutant General's office, Washington, March 27th, 1865, General Orders No. 50. Ordered, first: That at the hour of noon, on the 14th day of April, 1865, Brevet Major General Anderson will raise and plant upon the ruins of Fort Sumter, in Charleston Harbor, the same U. S. Flag which floated over the battlements of this fort during the rebel assault, and which was lowered and saluted by him and the small force of his command when the works were evacuated on the 14th day of April, 1861. Second, That the flag, when raised be saluted by 100 guns from Fort Sumter and by a national salute from every fort and rebel battery that fired upon Fort Sumter. Third, That suitable ceremonies be had upon the occasion, under the direction of Major-General William T. Sherman, whose military operations compelled the rebels to evacuate Charleston, or, in his absence, under the charge of Major-General Q. A. Gillmore, commanding the department. Among the ceremonies will be the delivery of a public address by the Rev. Henry Ward Beecher. Fourth, That the naval forces at Charleston and their Commander on that station be invited to participate in the ceremonies of the occasion. By order of the President of the United States. E. M. Stanton, Secretary of War."

April, 1865.—What a month this has been. On the 6th of April Governor Fenton issued this proclamation: "Richmond has fallen. The wicked men who governed the so-called Confederate States have fled their capital, shorn of their power and influence. The rebel armies have been defeated, broken and scattered. Victory everywhere attends our banners and our armies, and we are rapidly moving to the closing scenes of the war. Through the self-sacrifice and heroic devotion of our soldiers, the life of the republic has been saved and the American Union preserved. I, Reuben E. Fenton, Governor of the State of New York, do designate Friday, the 14th of April, the day appointed for the ceremony of raising the United States flag on Fort Sumter, as a day of Thanksgiving, prayer and praise to Almighty God, for the signal blessings we have received at His hands."

Saturday, April 8.—The cannon has fired a salute of thirty-six guns to celebrate the fall of Richmond. This evening the streets were thronged with men, women and children all acting crazy as if they had not the remotest idea where they were or what they were doing. Atwater block was beautifully lighted and the band was playing in front of it. On the square they fired guns, and bonfires were lighted in the streets. Gov. Clark's house was lighted from the very garret and they had a transparency in front, with " Richmond " on it, which Fred Thompson made. We didn't even light " our other candle," for Grandmother said she preferred to keep Saturday night and pity and pray for the poor suffering, wounded soldiers, who are so apt to be forgotten in the hour of victory.

Sunday Evening, April 9.—There were great crowds at church this morning.   Dr. Daggett's text was from Prov. 18: 10:   " The name of the Lord is a strong tower; the righteous runneth into it, and is safe." It was a very fine sermon.   They sang hymns relating to our country and Dr. Daggett's prayers were full of thanksgiving.   Mr. Noah T. Clarke had the chapel decorated with flags and opened the Sunday School by singing, " Marching On," " My Country, 'tis of Thee," " The Star Spangled Banner," " Glory, Hallelujah," etc.   Hon. Wm. H. Lamport talked very pleasantly and paid a very touching tribute to the memory of the boys, who had gone out to defend their country, who would never come " marching home again." He lost his only son, 18 years old (in the 126th), about two years ago.   I sat near Mary and Emma Wheeler and felt so sorry for them.   They could not sing.

Monday Morning, April 10.—" Whether I am in the body, or out of the body, I know not, but one thing I know," Lee has surrendered! and all the people seem crazy in consequence.   The bells are ringing, boys and girls, men and women are running through the streets wild with excitement; the flags are all flying, one from the top of our church, and such a " hurrah boys " generally, I never dreamed of. We were quietly eating our breakfast this morning about 7 o'clock, when our church bell commenced to ring, then the Methodist bell, and now all the bells in town are ringing. Mr. Noah T. Clarke ran by, all excitement, and I don't believe he knows where he is. No school to-day. I saw Capt. Aldrich passing, so I rushed to the window and he waved his hat. I raised the window and asked him what was the matter? He came to the front door where I met him and he almost shook my hand off and said, " The war is over. We have Lee's surrender, with his own name signed." I am going down town now, to see for myself, what is going on. Later—I have returned and I never saw such performances in my life. Every man has a bell or a horn, and every girl a flag and a little bell, and every one is tied with red, white and blue ribbons. I am going down town again now, with my flag in one hand and bell in the other and make all the noise I can. Mr. Noah T. Clarke and other leading citizens are riding around on a dray cart with great bells in their hands ringing them as hard as they can. Dr. Cook beat upon an old gong. The latest musical instrument invented is called the " Jerusalem fiddle." Some boys put a dry goods box upon a cart, put some rosin on the edge of the box and pulled a piece of timber back and forth across it, making most unearthly sounds. They drove through all the streets, Ed Lampman riding on the horse and driving it.

Monday evening, April 10.—I have been out walking for the last hour and a half, looking at the brilliant illuminations, transparencies and everything else and I don't believe I was ever so tired in my life. The bells have not stopped ringing more than five minutes all day and every one is glad to see Canandaigua startled out of its propriety for once. Every yard of red, white and blue ribbon in the stores has been sold, also every candle and every flag. One society worked hard all the afternoon making transparencies and then there were no candles to put in to light them, but they will be ready for the next celebration when peace is proclaimed. The Court House, Atwater Block, and hotel have about two dozen candles in each window throughout, besides flags and mottoes of every description. It is certainly the best impromptu display ever gotten up in this town. "Victory is Grant-ed," is in large red, white and blue letters in front of Atwater Block. The speeches on the square this morning were all very good. Dr. Daggett commenced with prayer, and such a prayer, I wish all could have heard it. Hon. Francis Granger, E. G. Lapham, Judge Smith, Alexander Howell, Noah T. Clarke and others made speeches and we sang "Old Hundred" in conclusion, and Rev. Dr. Hibbard dismissed us with the benediction. I shook hands with

Mr. Noah T. Clarke, but he told me to be careful and not hurt him, for he blistered his hands to-day ringing that bell. He says he is going to keep the bell for his grandchildren. Between the speeches on the square this morning a song was called for and Gus Coleman mounted the steps and started " John Brown " and all the assembly joined in the chorus, " Glory, Hallelujah." This has been a never to be forgotten day.

April 15.—The news came this morning that our dear president, Abraham Lincoln, was assassinated yesterday, on the day appointed for thanksgiving for Union victories. I have felt sick over it all day and so has every one that I have seen. All seem to feel as though they had lost a personal friend, and tears flow plenteously. How soon has sorrow followed upon the heels of joy! One week ago to-night we were celebrating our victories with loud acclamations of mirth and good cheer. Now every one is silent and sad and the earth and heavens seem clothed in sack-cloth. The bells have been tolling this afternoon. The flags are all at half mast, draped with mourning, and on every store and dwelling-house some sign of the nation's loss is visible. Just after breakfast this morning, I looked out of the window and saw a group of men listening to the reading of a morning paper, and I feared from their silent, motionless interest that something dreadful had happened, but I was not prepared to

hear of the cowardly murder of our President.
And William H. Seward, too, I suppose cannot survive his wounds.   Oh, how horrible it is!   I went
down town shortly after I heard the news, and it
was wonderful to see the effect of the intelligence
upon everybody, small or great, rich or poor.
Every one was talking low, with sad and anxious
looks.   But we know that God still reigns and will
do what is best for us all.   Perhaps we're " putting
our trust too much in princes," forgetting the Great
Ruler, who alone can create or destroy, and therefore He has taken from us the arm of flesh that
we may lean more confidingly and entirely upon
Him.   I   trust   that   the   men   who   committed
these foul deeds will soon be brought to justice.

Sunday, Easter Day, April 16.—I went to church
this morning.   The pulpit and choir-loft were covered with flags festooned with crape.   Although a
very disagreeable day, the house was well filled.
The first hymn sung was " Oh God our help in ages
past, our hope for years to come."   Dr. Daggett's
prayer, I can never forget, he alluded so beautifully
to the nation's loss, and prayed so fervently that the
God of our fathers might still be our God, through
every calamity or affliction, however severe or mysterious.   All seemed as deeply affected as though
each one had been suddenly bereft of his best
friend.   The hymn sung after the prayer, com-

menced with " Yes, the Redeemer rose." Dr. Daggett said that he had intended to preach a sermon upon the resurrection. He read the psalm beginning, " Lord, Thou hast been our dwelling-place in all generations." His text was " That our faith and hope might be in God." He commenced by saying, " I feel as you feel this morning: our sad hearts have all throbbed in unison since yesterday morning when the telegram announced to us Abraham Lincoln is shot." He said the last week would never be forgotten, for never had any of us seen one come in with so much joy, that went out with so much sorrow. His whole sermon related to the President's life and death, and, in conclusion, he exhorted us not to be despondent, for he was confident that the ship of state would not go down, though the helmsman had suddenly been taken away while the promised land was almost in view. He prayed for our new President, that he might be filled with grace and power from on High, to perform his high and holy trust. On Thursday we are to have a union meeting in our church, but it will not be the day of general rejoicing and thanksgiving we expected. All noisy demonstrations will be omitted. In Sunday school the desk was draped with mourning, and the flag at half-mast was also festooned with crape. Mr. Noah T. Clarke opened the exercises with the hymn " He leadeth me," followed by " Though the days are dark with sorrow," " We know not what's before us," " My days are gliding swiftly by." Then, Mr. Clarke said that we always meant to sing " America," after every victory, and last Monday he was wondering if we would not have to sing it twice to-day, or add another verse, but our feelings have changed since then. Nevertheless he thought we had better sing " America," for we certainly ought to love our country more than ever, now that another, and such another, martyr, had given up his life for it. So we sang it. Then he talked to the children and said that last Friday was supposed to be the anniversary of the day upon which our Lord was crucified, and though, at the time the dreadful deed was committed, every one felt the day to be the darkest one the earth ever knew; yet since then, the day has been called " Good Friday," for it was the death of Christ which gave life everlasting to all the people. So he thought that life would soon come out of darkness, which now overshadows us all, and that the death of Abraham Lincoln might yet prove the nation's life in God's own most mysterious way.

Wednesday evening, April 19, 1865.—This being the day set for the funeral of Abraham Lincoln at Washington, it was decided to hold the service to-day, instead of Thursday, as previously announced in the Congregational church. All places of business were closed and the bells of the village churches tolled from half past ten till eleven o'clock. It is

the fourth anniversary of the first bloodshed of the
war at Baltimore. It was said to-day, that while
the services were being held in the White House
and Lincoln's body lay in state under the dome
of the capitol, that more than twenty-five millions
of people all over the civilized world were gathered
in their churches weeping over the death of the mar-
tyred President. We met at our church at half
after ten o'clock this morning. The bells tolled
until eleven o'clock, when the services commenced.
The church was beautifully decorated with flags
and black and white cloth, wreaths, mottoes and
flowers, the galleries and all. The whole effect
was fine. There was a shield beneath the arch
of the pulpit with this text upon it: " The memory of the just is blessed." It was beautiful.
Under the choir-loft the picture of Abraham
Lincoln hung amid the flags and drapery. The
motto, beneath the gallery, was this text: " Know
ye that the Lord He is God." The four pastors
of the place walked in together and took seats upon
the platform, which was constructed for the occasion. The choir chanted " Lord, Thou hast been
our dwelling-place in all generations," and then the
Episcopal rector, Rev. Mr. Leffingwell, read from
the psalter, and Rev. Dr. Daggett followed with
prayer. Judge Taylor was then called upon for
a short address, and he spoke well, as he always
does. The choir sang " God is our refuge and our
strength."

Thursday, April 20.—The papers are full of the account of the funeral obsequies of President Lincoln. We take Harper's Weekly and every event is pictured so vividly it seems as though we were eye witnesses of it all. The picture of " Lincoln at home " is beautiful. What a dear, kind man he was. It is a comfort to know that the assassination was not the outcome of an organized plot of Southern leaders, but rather a conspiracy of a few fanatics, who undertook in this way to avenge the defeat of their cause. It is rumored that one of the conspirators has been located.

April 24.—Fannie Gaylord and Kate Lapham have returned from their eastern trip and told us of attending the President's funeral in Albany, and I had a letter from Bessie Seymour, who is in New York, saying that she walked in the procession until half past two in the morning, in order to see his face. They say that they never saw him in life, but in death he looked just as all the pictures represent him. We all wear Lincoln badges now, with pin attached. They are pictures of Lincoln upon a tiny flag, bordered with crape. Susie Daggett has just made herself a flag, six feet by four. It was a lot of work. Mrs. Noah T. Clarke gave one to her husband upon his birthday, April 8. I think everybody ought to own a flag.

April 26.—Now we have the news that J. Wilkes Booth, who shot the President and who has been concealing himself in Virginia, has been caught, and refusing to surrender was shot dead. It has taken just twelve days to bring him to retribution. I am glad that he is dead if he could not be taken alive, but it seems as though shooting was too good for him. However, we may as well take this as really God's way, as the death of the President, for if he had been taken alive, the country would have been so furious to get at him and tear him to pieces the turmoil would have been great and desperate. It may be the best way to dispose of him. Of course, it is best, or it would not be so. Mr. Morse called this evening and he thinks Booth was shot by a lot of cowards. The flags have been flying all day, since the news came, but all, excepting Albert Granger, seem sorry that he was not disabled instead of being shot dead. Albert seems able to look into the "beyond" and also to locate departed spirits. His "latest" is that he is so glad that Booth got to h—l before Abraham Lincoln got to Springfield.

Mr. Fred Thompson went down to New York last Saturday and while stopping a few minutes at St. Johnsville, he heard a man crowing over the death of the President. Mr. Thompson marched up to him, collared him and landed him nicely in the gutter. The bystanders were delighted and carried the champion to a platform and called for a speech, which was given. Quite a little episode. Every one who hears the story, says: "Three cheers for F. F. Thompson."

The other afternoon at our society Kate Lapham wanted to divert our minds from gossip I think, and so started a discussion upon the respective characters of Washington and Napoleon. It was just after supper and Laura Chapin was about resuming her sewing and she exclaimed, " Speaking of Washington, makes me think that I ought to wash my hands," so she left the room for that purpose.

May 7.—Anna and I wore our new poke bonnets to church this morning and thought we looked quite " scrumptious," but Grandmother said after we got home, if she had realized how unbecoming they were to us and to the house of the Lord, she could not have countenanced them enough to have sat in the same pew. However, she tried to agree with Dr. Daggett in his text, " It is good for us to be here." It was the first time in a month that he had not preached about the affairs of the Nation.

In the afternoon the Sacrament was administered and Rev. A. D. Eddy, D. D., who was pastor from 1823 to 1835, was present and officiated. Deacon Castle and Deacon Hayes passed the communion. Dr. Eddy concluded the services with some personal memories. He said that forty-two years ago last November, he presided upon a similar occasion for the first time in his life and it was in this very church. He is now the only surviving male member who was present that day, but there are six women living, and Grandmother is one of the six.

The Monthly Concert of Prayer for Missions was held in the chapel in the evening. Dr. Daggett told us that the collection taken for missions during the past year amounted to $500. He commended us and said it was the largest sum raised in one year for this purpose in the twenty years of his pastorate. Dr. Eddy then said that in contrast he would tell us that the collection for missions the first year he was here, amounted to $5, and that he was advised to touch very lightly upon the subject in his appeals as it was not a popular theme with the majority of the people. One member, he said, annexed three ciphers to his name when asked to subscribe to a missionary document which was circulated, and another man replied thus to an appeal for aid in evangelizing a portion of Asia: " If you want to send a missionary to Jerusalem, Yates county, I will contribute, but not a cent to go to the other side of the world."

Rev. C. H. A. Buckley was present also and gave an interesting talk. By way of illustration, he said he knew a small boy who had been earning twenty-five cents a week for the heathen by giving up eating butter. The other day he seemed to think that his generosity, as well as his self-denial, had reached the utmost limit and exclaimed as he sat at the table, " I think the heathen have had gospel enough, please pass the butter."

May 10.—Jeff Davis was captured to-day at
Irwinsville, Ga., when he was attempting to escape
in woman's apparel. Mr. Green drew a picture
of him, and Mr. Finley made photographs
from it. We bought one as a souvenir of the
war.

The big headlines in the papers this morning say,
" The hunt is up. He brandisheth a bowie-knife
but yieldeth to six solid arguments. At Irwinsville,
Ga., about daylight on the 10th instant, Col. Prich-
ard, commanding the 4th Michigan Cavalry, captured Jeff Davis, family and staff. They will be
forwarded under strong guard without delay."
The flags have been flying all day, and every one
is about as pleased over the manner of his capture
as over the fact itself. Lieutenant Hathaway, one
of the staff, is a friend of Mr. Manning Wells, and
he was pretty sure he would follow Davis, so we
were not surprised to see his name among the captured. Mr. Wells says he is as fine a horseman as
he ever saw.

Monday evg., May 22.—I went to Teachers'
meeting at Mrs. Worthington's to-night. Mrs.
George Willson is the leader and she told us at the
last meeting to be prepared this evening to give our
opinion in regard to the repentance of Solomon before he died. We concluded that he did repent
although the Bible does not absolutely say so.
Grandmother thinks such questions are unprofitable,

as we would better be repenting of our sins, instead of hunting up Solomon's at this late day.

May 23.—We arise about 5:30 nowadays and Anna does not like it very well. I asked her why she was not as good natured as usual to-day and she said it was because she got up " s'urly." She thinks Solomon must have been acquainted with Grandmother when he wrote " She ariseth while it is yet night and giveth meat to her household and a portion to her maidens." Patrick Burns, the " poet," who has also been our man of all work the past year, has left us to go into Mr. McKechnie's employ. He seemed to feel great regret when he bade us farewell and told us he never lived in a better regulated home than ours and he hoped his successor would take the same interest in us that he had. Perhaps he will give us a recommendation! He left one of his poems as a souvenir. It is entitled, " There will soon be an end to the war," written in March, hence a prophecy. He said Mr. Morse had read it and pronounced it " tip top." It was mostly written in capitals and I asked him if he followed any rule in regard to their use. He said " Oh, yes, always begin a line with one and then use your own discretion with the rest."

May 25.—I wish that I could have been in Washington this week, to have witnessed the grand review of Meade's and Sherman's armies. The newspaper accounts are most thrilling. The review commenced on Tuesday morning and lasted two days. It took over six hours for Meade's army to pass the grand stand, which was erected in front of the President's house. It was witnessed by the President, Generals Grant, Meade, and Sherman, Secretary Stanton, and many others in high authority. At ten o'clock, Wednesday morning, Sherman's army commenced to pass in review. His men did not show the signs of hardship and suffering which marked the appearance of the Army of the Potomac. The scenes enacted were historic and wonderful. Flags were flying everywhere and windows, doorsteps and sidewalks were crowded with people, eager to get a view of the grand armies. The city was as full of strangers, who had come to see the sight, as on Inauguration Day. Very soon, all that are left of the companies, who went from here, will be marching home, " with glad and gallant tread."

June 3.—I was invited up to Sonnenberg yesterday and Lottie and Abbie Clark called for me at 5:30 P.M., with their pony and democrat wagon. Jennie Rankine was the only other lady present and, for a wonder, the party consisted of six gentlemen and five ladies, which has not often been the case during the war. After supper we adjourned to the lawn and played croquet, a new game which Mr. Thompson just brought from New York. It is

something like billiards, only a mallet is used instead
of a cue to hit the balls. I did not like it very
well, because I couldn't hit the balls through the
wickets as I wanted to. " We " sang all the songs,
patriotic and sentimental, that we could think of.

Mr. Lyon came to call upon me to-day, before he
returned to New York. He is a very pleasant
young man. I told him that I regretted that I could
not sing yesterday, when all the others did, and
that the reason that I made no attempts in that line
was due to the fact that one day in church, when
I thought I was singing a very good alto, my grandfather whispered to me, and said: " Daughter,
you are off the key," and ever since then, I had sung
with the spirit and with the understanding, but not
with my voice. He said perhaps I could get some
one to do my singing for me, some day. I told him
he was very kind to give me so much encouragement.
Anna went to a Y.M.C.A. meeting last evening at
our chapel and said, when the hymn " Rescue the
perishing," was given out, she just " raised her
Ebenezer " and sang every verse as hard as she
could. The meeting was called in behalf of a
young man who has been around town for the past
few days, with only one arm, who wants to be a minister and sells sewing silk and needles and writes
poetry during vacation to help himself along. I have
had a cough lately and Grandmother decided yesterday to send for the doctor. He placed me in a chair
and thumped my lungs and back and listened to my

breathing while Grandmother sat near and watched him in silence, but finally she said, " Caroline isn't used to being pounded!" The doctor smiled and said he would be very careful, but the treatment was not so severe as it seemed. After he was gone, we asked Grandmother if she liked him and she said yes, but if she had known of his " new-fangled " notions and that he wore a full beard she might not have sent for him! Because Dr. Carr was clean-shaven and also Grandfather and Dr. Daggett, and all of the Grangers, she thinks that is the only proper way. What a funny little lady she is!

June 8.—There have been unusual attractions down town for the past two days. About 5 P.M. a man belonging to the Ravel troupe walked a rope, stretched across Main street from the third story of the Webster House to the chimney of the building opposite. He is said to be Blondin's only rival and certainly performed some extraordinary feats. He walked across and then returned backwards. Then took a wheel-barrow across and returned with it backwards. He went across blindfolded with a bag over his head. Then he attached a short trapeze to the rope and performed all sorts of gymnastics. There were at least 1,000 people in the street and in the windows gazing at him. Grandmother says that she thinks all such performances are wicked, tempting Providence to win the applause of men. Nothing would induce her to look upon

such things. She is a born reformer and would
abolish all such schemes. This morning she wanted
us to read the 11th chapter of Hebrews to her, about
faith, and when we had finished the forty verses,
Anna asked her what was the difference between
her and Moses. Grandmother said there were many
points of difference. Anna was not found in the
bulrushes and she was not adopted by a king's
daughter. Anna said she was thinking how the
verse read, " Moses was a proper child," and she
could not remember having ever done anything
strictly " proper " in her life. I noticed that Grandmother did not contradict her, but only smiled.

June 13.—Van Amburgh's circus was in town
to-day and crowds attended and many of our most
highly respected citizens, but Grandmother had
other things for us to consider.

June 16.—The census man for this town is Mr.
Jeudevine. He called here to-day and was very in-
quisitive, but I think I answered all of his questions although I could not tell him the exact amount
of my property. Grandmother made us laugh to-
day when we showed her a picture of the Siamese
twins, and I said, " Grandmother, if I had been
their mother I should have cut them apart when they
were babies, wouldn't you? " The dear little lady
looked up so bright and said, " If I had been Mrs.
Siam, I presume I should have done just as she did."

I don't believe that we will be as amusing as she is when we are 82 years old.

Saturday, July 8.—What excitement there must have been in Washington yesterday over the execution of the conspirators.   It seems terrible that Mrs. Surratt should have deserved hanging with the others.   I saw a picture of them all upon a scaffold and her face was screened by an umbrella.   I read in one paper that the doctor who dressed Booth's broken leg was sentenced to the Dry Tortugas. Jefferson Davis, I suppose, is glad to have nothing worse served upon him, thus far, than confinement in Fortress Monroe.   It is wonderful that 800,000 men are returning so quietly from the army to civil life that it is scarcely known, save by the welcome which they receive in their own homes.

July 16.—Rev. Dr. Buddington, of Brooklyn, preached to-day.   His wife was Miss Elizabeth Willson, Clara Coleman's sister.   My Sunday School book is " Mill on the Floss," but Grandmother says it is not Sabbath reading, so I am stranded for the present.

December 8.—Yesterday was Thanksgiving day. I do not remember that it was ever observed in December before.   President Johnson appointed it as a day of national thanksgiving for our many blessings as a people, and Governor Fenton and several governors of other states have issued proclamations in accordance with the President's recommendation. The weather was very unpleasant, but we attended the union thanksgiving service held in our church. The choir sang America for the opening piece. Dr. Daggett read Miriam's song of praise: " The Lord hath triumphed gloriously, the horse and his rider hath he thrown into the sea." Then he offered one of his most eloquent and fervent prayers, in which the returned soldiers, many of whom are in broken health or maimed for life, in consequence of their devotion and loyalty to their country, were tenderly remembered. His text was from the 126th Psalm, " The Lord hath done great things for us, whereof we are glad." It was one of his best sermons. He mentioned three things in particular which the Lord has done for us, whereof we are glad: First, that the war has closed; second, that the Union is preserved; third, for the abolition of slavery. After the sermon, a collection was taken for the poor, and Dr. A. D. Eddy, who was present, offered prayer. The choir sang an anthem which they had especially prepared for the occasion, and then all joined in the doxology. Uncle Thomas Beals' family of four united with our three at Thanksgiving dinner. Uncle sent to New York for the oysters, and a famous big turkey, with all the usual accompaniments, made us a fine repast. Anna and Ritie Tyler are reading together

Irving's Life of Washington, two afternoons each
week.   I wonder how long they will keep it up.

December 11.—I have been down town buying
material for garments for our Home Missionary
family which we are to make in our society.   Anna
and I were cutting them out and basting them ready
for sewing, and grandmother told us to save all the
basting threads when we were through with them
and tie them and wind them on a spool for use another time.   Anna, who says she never wants to begin anything that she cannot finish in 15 minutes,
felt rather tired at the prospect of this unexpected
task and asked Grandmother how she happened to
contract such economical ideas.   Grandmother told
her that if she and Grandfather had been wasteful
in their younger days, we would not have any silk
dresses to wear now.   Anna said if that was the
case she was glad that Grandmother saved the basting thread!

1866

February 13.—Our brother James was married to-day to Louise Livingston James of New York City.

February 20.—Our society is going to hold a fair for the Freedmen, in the Town Hall. Susie Daggett and I have been there all day to see about the tables and stoves. We got Mrs. Binks to come and help us.

February 21.—Been at the hall all day, trimming the room. Mr. Thompson and Mr. Backus came down and if they had not helped us we would not have done much. Mr. Backus put up all the principal drapery and made it look beautiful.

February 22.—At the hall all day. The fair opened at 2 P.M. We had quite a crowd in the evening and took in over three hundred dollars. Charlie Hills and Ellsworth Daggett stayed there all night to take care of the hall. We had a fish pond, a grab-bag and a post-office. Anna says they had all the smart people in the post-office to write the letters,—Mr. Morse, Miss Achert, Albert Granger and herself. Some one asked Albert

Granger if his law business was good and he said one man thronged into his office one day.

February 23.—We took in two hundred dollars to-day at the fair. We wound up with an auction. We asked Mrs. George Willson if she could not write a poem expressing our thanks to Mr. Backus and she stepped aside for about five minutes and handed us the following lines which we sent to him. We think it is about the nicest thing in the whole fair.

> " In ancient time the God of Wine
> They crowned with vintage of the vine,
> And sung his praise with song and glee
> And all their best of minstrelsy.
> The Backus whom we honor now
> Would scorn to wreathe his generous brow
> With heathen emblems—better he
> Will love our gratitude to see
> Expressed in all the happy faces
> Assembled in these pleasant places.
> May joy attend his footsteps here
> And crown him in a brighter sphere."

February 24.—Susie Daggett and I went to the hall this morning to clean up. We sent back the dishes, not one broken, and disposed of everything but the tables and stoves, which were to be taken away this afternoon. We feel quite satisfied with the receipts so far, but the expenses will be considerable.

In *Ontario County Times* of the following week we find this card of thanks:

February 28.—The Fair for the benefit of the
Freedmen, held in the Town Hall on Thursday and
Friday of last week was eminently successful, and
the young ladies take this method of returning their
sincere thanks to the people of Canandaigua and
vicinity for their generous contributions and liberal
patronage.   It being the first public enterprise in
which the Society has ventured independently, the
young ladies were somewhat fearful of the result,
but having met with such generous responses from
every quarter they feel assured that they need never
again doubt of success in any similar attempt so
long as Canandaigua contains so many large hearts
and corresponding purses.   But our village cannot
have all the praise this time.   The Society is particularly indebted to Mr. F. F. Thompson and Mr.
S. D. Backus of New York City, for their very substantial aid, not only in gifts and unstinted patronage, but for their invaluable labor in the decoration
of the hall and conduct of the Fair.   But for them
most of the manual labor would have fallen upon
the ladies.   The thanks of the Society are especially due, also, to those ladies who assisted personally with their superior knowledge and older
experience.   Also to Mr. W. P. Fiske for his valuable services as cashier, and to Messrs. Daggett,
Chapin and Hills for services at the door; and to all
the little boys and girls who helped in so many ways.

The receipts amounted to about $490, and thanks
to our cashier, the money is all good, and will soon

be on its way carrying substantial visions of something to eat and to wear to at least a few of the poor Freedmen of the South.

By order of Society,

CARRIE C. RICHARDS, *Pres't.*

EMMA H. WHEELER, *Sec'y.*

MR. EDITOR—I expected to see an account of the Young Ladies' Fair in your last number, but only saw a very handsome acknowledgment by the ladies to the citizens. Your " local " must have been absent; and I beg the privilege in behalf of myself and many others of doing tardy justice to the successful efforts of the Aid Society at their debut February 22nd.

Gotham furnished an artist and an architect, and the Society did the rest. The decorations were in excellent taste, and so were the young ladies. The eatables were very toothsome. The skating pond was never in better condition. On entering the hall I paused first before the table of toys, fancy work and perfumery. Here was the President, and I hope I shall be pardoned for saying that no President since the days of Washington can compare with the President of this Society. Then I visited a candy table, and hesitated a long time before deciding which I would rather eat, the delicacies that were sold, or the charming creatures who sold them. One delicious morsel, in a pink silk, was so tempting that I seriously contemplated eating her with a spoon—waterfall and all. [By the way, how do we know that the Romans wore waterfalls? Because Marc Antony, in his funeral oration on Mr. Cæsar, exclaimed, " O water fall was there, my countrymen! "] At this point my attention was attracted by a fish pond. I tried my luck, caught a whale, and seeing all my friends beginning to blubber, I determined to visit the old woman who lived in a shoe.—She was very glad to see me. I bought one of her children, which the Society can redeem for $1,000 in smoking caps.

The fried oysters were delicious; a great many of the bivalves got into a stew, and I helped several of them out. Delicate ice cream, nicely "baked in cowld ovens," was destroyed in immense quantities. I scream when I remember the plates full I devoured, and the number of bright women to whom I paid my devours. Beautiful cigar girls sold fragrant Havanas, and bit off the ends at five cents apiece, extra. The fair post-mistress and her fair clerks, so fair that they were almost fairies, drove a very thriving business.

It was altogether a " great moral show."—Let no man say hereafter that the young ladies of Canandaigua are uneducated in all that makes women lovely and useful. Anna Dickinson has no mission to this town. The members of this Society have won the admiration of all their friends, and especially of the most devoted of their servants,   Q. E. D.

If I had written that article, I should have given the praise to Susie Daggett, for it belongs to her.

Sunday, June 24.—My Sunday School scholars are learning the shorter catechism. One recited thirty-five answers to questions to-day, another twenty-six, another twenty, the others eleven. Very well indeed. They do not see why it is called the " shorter " Catechism! They all had their ambrotypes taken with me yesterday at Finley's—Mary

Hoyt, Fannie and Ella Lyon, Ella Wood, Ella Van
Tyne, Mary Vanderbrook, Jennie Whitlaw and
Katie Neu. They are all going to dress in white
and sit on the front seat in church at my wedding.
Grandmother had Mrs. Gooding make individual
fruit cakes for each of them and also some for each
member of our sewing society.

Thursday, June 21.—We went to a lawn fete at
Mrs. F. F. Thompson's this afternoon. It was a
beautiful sight. The flowers, the grounds, the
young people and the music all combined to make
the occasion perfect.

Note: Canandaigua is the summer home of Mrs.
Thompson, who has previously given the village a
children's playground, a swimming school, a hospital
and a home for the aged, and this year (1911) has presented a park as a beauty spot at foot of Canandaigua
Lake.

June 28.—Dear Abbie Clark and Captain Williams were married in the Congregational church
this evening. The church was trimmed beautifully
and Abbie looked sweet. We attended the reception afterwards at her house. " May calm and sun-
shine hallow their clasped hands."

July 15.—The girls of the Society have sent me
my flag bed quilt, which they have just finished. It
was hard work quilting such hot days but it is done

beautifully. Bessie Seymour wrote the names on the stars. In the center they used six stars for "Three rousing cheers for the Union." The names on the others are Sarah McCabe, Mary Paul, Fannie Paul, Fannie Palmer, Nettie Palmer, Susie Daggett, Fannie Pierce, Sarah Andrews, Lottie Clark, Abbie Williams, Carrie Lamport, Isadore Blodgett, Nannie Corson, Laura Chapin, Mary F. Fiske, Lucilla F. Pratt, Jennie H. Hazard, Sarah H. Foster, Mary Jewett, Mary C. Stevens, Etta Smith, Cornelia Richards, Ella Hildreth, Emma Wheeler, Mary Wheeler, Mrs. Pierce, Alice Jewett, Bessie Seymour, Clara Coleman, Julia Phelps. It kept the girls busy to get Abbie Clark's quilt and mine finished within one month. They hope that the rest of the girls will postpone their nuptials till there is a change in the weather. Mercury stands 90 degrees in the shade.

July 19, 1866.—Our wedding day. We saw the dear little Grandmother, God bless her, watching us from the window as we drove away.

ALEXANDRIA BAY, *July* 26.—Anna writes me that Charlie Wells said he had always wanted a set of Clark's Commentaries, but I had carried off the entire Ed.

July 28.—As we were changing boats at Burlington, Vt., for Saratoga, to our surprise, we met Captain and Abbie Williams, but could only stop a moment.

SARATOGA, 29th.—We heard Rev. Theodore Cuyler preach to-day from the text, " Demas hath forsaken me, having loved this present world." He leads devotional exercises every morning in the parlors of the Columbian Hotel. I spoke to him this morning and he said my father was one of his best and earliest friends.

CANANDAIGUA, September 1.—A party of us went down to the Canandaigua hotel this morning to see President Johnson, General Grant and Admiral Farragut and other dignitaries. The train stopped about half an hour and they all gave brief speeches.

September 2.—Rev. Darius Sackett preached for Dr. Daggett this evening.

1867

July 27.—Col. James M. Bull was buried from the home of Mr. Alexander Howell to-day, as none of his family reside here now.

November 13.—Our brother John and wife and baby Pearl have gone to London, England, to live.

December 28.—A large party of Canandaiguans went over to Rochester last evening to hear Charles Dickens' lecture, and enjoyed it more than I can possibly express. He was quite hoarse and had small bills distributed through the Opera House with the announcement:

MR. CHARLES DICKENS

Begs indulgence for a Severe Cold, but hopes its effects may not be very perceptible after a few minutes' Reading.
Friday, December 27th, 1867.

We brought these notices home with us for souvenirs. He looks exactly like his pictures. It was worth a great deal just to look upon the man who wrote Little Dorrit, David Copperfield and all the other books, which have delighted us so much. We hope that he will live to write a great many more. He spoke very appreciatively of his enthusiastic reception in this country and almost apologized for some of the opinions that he had expressed in his " American Notes," which he published, after his first visit here, twenty-five years ago.   He evidently thinks that the United States of America are quite worth while.

1871

August 6.—Under the auspices of the Y.M.C.A., Hon. George H. Stuart, President of the U. S. Christian Commission, spoke in an open air meeting on the square this afternoon and in our church this evening. The house was packed and such eloquence I never heard from mortal lips. He ought to be called the Whitefield of America. He told of the good the Christian Commission had done before the war and since. Such war stories I never heard. They took up a collection which must have amounted to hundreds of dollars.

1872

Naples, June.—John has invited Aunt Ann Field, and James, his wife and me and Babe Abigail to come to England to make them a visit, and we expect to sail on the Baltic July sixth.

On board S.S. Baltic, July 7.—We left New York yesterday under favorable circumstances. It was a beautiful summer day, flags were flying and everything seemed so joyful we almost forgot we were leaving home and native land. There were many passengers, among them being Mr. and Mrs. Anthony Drexel and U. S. Grant, Jr., who boarded the steamer from a tug boat which came down the bay alongside when we had been out half an hour. President Grant was with him and stood on deck, smoking the proverbial cigar. We were glad to see him and the passengers gave him three cheers and three times three, with the greatest enthusiasm.

Liverpool, July 16.—We arrived here to-day, having been just ten days on the voyage. There were many clergymen of note on board, among them, Rev. John H. Vincent, D.D., eminent in the Methodist Episcopal Church, who is preparing International Sunday School lessons. He sat at our table and Philip Phillips also, who is a noted evangelistic singer. They held services both Sabbaths, July 7 and 15, in the grand saloon of the steamer, and also in the steerage where the text was " And they willingly received him into the ship." The immigrants listened eagerly, when the minister urged them all to " receive Jesus." We enjoyed several evening literary entertainments, when it was too cold or windy to sit on deck.

We had the most luscious strawberries at dinner to-night, that I ever ate. So large and red and ripe, with the hulls on and we dipped them in powdered sugar as we ate them, a most appetizing way.

London, July 17.—On our way to London to-day I noticed beautiful flower beds at every station, making our journey almost a path of roses. In the fields, men and women both, were harvesting the hay, making picturesque scenes, for the sky was cloudless and I was reminded of the old hymn, commencing

> "Sweet fields beyond the swelling flood,
> Stand dressed in living green."

We performed the journey from Liverpool to London, a distance of 240 miles, in five hours. John, Laura and little Pearl met us at Euston Station, and we were soon whirled away in cabs to 24 Upper Woburn Place, Tavistock Square, John's residence. Dinner was soon ready, a most bountiful repast. We spent the remainder of the day visiting and enjoying ourselves generally. It seemed so good to be at the end of the journey, although we had only two days of really unpleasant weather on the voyage. John and Laura are so kind and hospitable. They have a beautiful home, lovely children and apparently every comfort and luxury which this world can afford.

Sunday, July 22.—We went to Spurgeon's Tabernacle this morning to listen to this great preacher, with thousands of others. I had never looked upon such a sea of faces before, as I beheld from the gallery where we sat. The pulpit was underneath one gallery, so there seemed as many people over the preacher's head, as there were beneath and around him and the singing was as impressive as the sermon. I thought of the hymn, " Hark ten thousand harps and voices, Sound the notes of praise above." Mr. Spurgeon was so lame from rheumatism that he used two canes and placed one knee on a chair beside him, when preaching. His text was " And there shall be a new heaven and a new earth." I found that all I had heard of his eloquence was true.

Sunday, July 29.—We have spent the entire week sightseeing, taking in Hyde Park, Windsor Castle, Westminster Abbey, St. Paul's Cathedral, the Tower of London and British Museum. We also went to Madame Tussaud's exhibition of wax figures and while I was looking in the catalogue for the number of an old gentleman who was sitting down apparently asleep, he got up and walked away! We drove to Sydenham ten miles from London, to see the Crystal Palace which Abbie called the "Christmas Palace." Mr. Alexander Howell and Mr. Henry Chesebro of Canandaigua are here and came to see us to-day.

August 13.—Amid the whirl of visiting, shopping and sightseeing in this great city, my diary has been well nigh forgotten. The descriptive letters to home friends have been numerous and knowing that they would be preserved, I thought perhaps they would do as well for future reference as a diary kept for the same purpose, but to-day, as St. Pancras' bell was tolling and a funeral procession going by, we heard by cable of the death of our dear, dear Grandmother, the one who first encouraged us to keep a journal of daily deeds, and who was always most interested in all that interested us and now I cannot refrain if I would, from writing down at this sad hour, of all the grief that is in my heart. I sorrow not for her. She has only stepped inside the temple-gate where she has long been waiting for the Lord's entrance call. I weep for ourselves that we shall see her dear face no more. It does not seem possible that we shall never see her again on this earth. She took such an interest in our journey and just as we started I put my dear little Abigail Beals Clarke in her lap to receive her parting blessing. As we left the house she sat at the front window and saw us go and smiled her farewell.

August 20.—Anna has written how often Grandmother prayed that " He who holds the winds in his fists and the waters in the hollow of his hands, would care for us and bring us to our desired haven." She had received one letter, telling of our safe arrival and how much we enjoyed going about London, when she was suddenly taken ill and Dr. Hayes said she could never recover. Anna's letter came, after ten days, telling us all the sad news, and how Grandmother looked out of the window the last night before she was taken ill, and up at the moon and stars and said how beautiful they were. Anna says, " How can I ever write it? Our dear little Grandmother died on my bed to-day."

August 30.—John, Laura and their nurse and baby John, Aunt Ann Field and I started Tuesday on a trip to Scotland, going first to Glasgow where we remained twenty-four hours. We visited the Cathedral and were about to go down into the crypt when the guide told us that Gen. Sherman of U.S.A. was just coming in. We stopped to look at him and felt like telling him that we too were Americans. He was in good health and spirits, apparently, and looked every inch a soldier with his cloak a-la-militaire around him.   We visited the Lochs and spent one night at Inversnaid on Loch Lomond and then went on up Loch Katrine to the Trossachs.   When we took the little steamer, John said, " All aboard for Naples," it reminded him so much of Canandaigua Lake.   We arrived safely in Edinburgh the next day by rail and spent four days in that charming city, so beautiful in situation and in every natural advantage.   We saw the window from whence John Knox addressed the populace and we also visited the Castle on the hill.   Then we went to Melrose and visited the Abbey and also Abbotsford, the residence of Sir Walter Scott.   We went through the rooms and saw many curios and paintings and also the library.   Sir Walter's chair at his desk was protected by a rope, but Laura, nothing daunted, lifted the baby over it and seated him there for a moment saying " I am sure, now, he will be clever."   We continued our journey that night and arrived in London the next morning.

Ventnor, Isle of Wight, September 9.—Aunt Ann, Laura's sister, Florentine Arnold, nurse and two children, Pearl and Abbie, and I are here for three weeks on the seashore.

September 16.—We have visited all the neighboring towns, the graves of the Dairyman's daughter and little Jane, the young cottager, and the scene

of Leigh Richmond's life and labors.   We have enjoyed bathing in the surf, and the children playing
in the sands and riding on the donkeys.

We have very pleasant rooms, in a house kept by
an old couple, Mr. and Mrs. Tuddenham, down on
the esplanade.   They serve excellent meals in a most
homelike way.   We have an abundance of delicious
milk and cream which they tell me comes from
" Cowes "!

London, September 30.—Anna has come to England to live with John for the present.   She came
on the Adriatic, arriving September 24.   We are so
glad to see her once more and will do all in our
power to cheer her in her loneliness.

Paris, October 18.—John, Laura, Aunt Ann and
I, nurse and baby, arrived here to-day for a few
days' visit.   We had rather a stormy passage on
the Channel.   I asked one of the seamen the name
of the vessel and he answered me " The H'Albert
H'Edward, Miss!"   This information must have
given me courage, for I was perfectly sustained till
we reached Calais, although nearly every one around
me succumbed.

October 22.—We have driven through the Bois
de Boulogne, visited Père la Chaise, the Morgue, the
ruins of the Tuileries, which are left just as they
were since the Commune.   We spent half a day at

the Louvre without seeing half of its wonders. I
went alone to a photographer's, Le Jeune, to be
" taken " and had a funny time. He queried
" Parlez-vous Français? " I shook my head and
asked him " Parlez-vous Anglaise? " at which
query he shrugged his shoulders and shook his head!
I ventured to tell him by signs that I would like my
picture taken and he held up two sizes of pictures
and asked me " Le cabinet, le vignette? " I held
up my fingers, to tell him I would like six of each,
whereupon he proceeded to make ready and when
he had seated me, he made me understand that he
hoped I would sit perfectly still, which I endeavored
to do.   After the first sitting, he showed displeasure
and let me know that I had swayed to and fro.   Another attempt was more satisfactory and he said
" Très bien, Madame," and I gave him my address
and departed.

October 26.—My photographs have come and all
pronounce them indeed " très bien." We visited the
Tomb of Napoleon to-day.

October 27.—We attended service to-day at the
American Chapel and I enjoyed it more than I
can ever express. After hearing a foreign tongue
for the past ten days, it seemed like getting home to
go into a Presbyterian church and hear a sermon
from an American pastor. The singing in the
choir was so homelike, that when they sang " Awake

my soul to joyful lays and sing thy great Redeemer's praise," it seemed to me that I heard a well
known tenor voice from across the sea, especially
in the refrain " His loving kindness, oh how free."
The text was " As an eagle stirreth up her nest, flut-
tereth over her young, spreadeth abroad her wings,
taketh them, beareth them on her wings, so the
Lord did lead him and there was no strange God
with him." Deut. 32:11. It was a wonderful
sermon and I shall never forget it. On our way
home, we noticed the usual traffic going on, building
of houses, women were standing in their doors
knitting and there seemed to be no sign of Sunday
keeping, outside of the church.

London, October 31.—John and I returned together from Paris and now I have only a few days
left before sailing for home. There was an Eng-
lishman here to-day who was bragging about the
beer in England being so much better than could be
made anywhere else. He said, " In America, you
have the 'ops, I know, but you haven't the Thames
water, you know." I suppose that would make a
vast difference !

Sunday, November 3.—We went to hear Rev. Dr.
Joseph Parker preach at Exeter Hall. He is a new
light, comparatively, and bids fair to rival Spurgeon and Newman Hall and all the rest. He is
like a lion and again like a lamb in the pulpit.

Liverpool, November 6.—I came down to Liverpool to-day with Abbie and nurse, to sail on the Baltic, to-morrow. There were two Englishmen in our compartment and hearing Abbie sing " I have a Father in the Promised Land," they asked her where her Father lived and she said " In America," and told them she was going on the big ship to-morrow to see him. Then they turned to me and said they supposed I would be glad to know that the latest cable from America was that U. S. Grant was elected for his second term as President of the United States. I assured them that I was very glad to hear such good news.

November 9.—I did not know any of the passengers when we sailed, but soon made pleasant acquaintances. Near me at table are Mr. and Mrs. Sykes from New York and in course of conversation I found that she as well as myself, was born in Penn Yan, Yates County, New York, and that her parents were members of my Father's church, which goes to prove that the world is not so very wide after all. Abbie is a great pet among the passengers and is being passed around from one to another from morning till night. They love to hear her sing and coax her to say " Grace " at table. She closes her eyes and folds her hands devoutly and says, " For what we are about to receive, may the Lord make us truly thankful." They all say " Amen " to this, for they are fearful that they will not perhaps be "thankful" when they finish!

November 15.—I have been on deck every day but one, and not missed a single meal.   There was a terrible storm one night and the next morning I told one of the numerous clergymen, that I took great comfort in the night, thinking that nothing could happen with so many of the Lord's anointed, on board.   He said that he wished he had thought of that, for he was frightened almost to death!   We have sighted eleven steamers and on Wednesday we were in sight of the banks of Newfoundland all the afternoon, our course being unusually northerly and we encountered no fogs, contrary to the expectation of all.   Every one pronounces the voyage pleasant and speedy for this time of year.

Naples, N. Y., November 20.—We arrived safely in New York on Sunday.   Abbie spied her father very quickly upon the dock as we slowly came up and with glad and happy hearts we returned his "Welcome home."   We spent two days in New York and arrived home safe and sound this evening.

November 21.—My thirtieth birthday, which we, a reunited family, are spending happily together around our own fireside, pleasant memories of the past months adding to the joy of the hour.

From the *New York Evangelist* of August 15,
1872, by Rev. Samuel Pratt, D.D.

" Died, at Canandaigua, N. Y., August 8, 1872,
Mrs. Abigail Field Beals, widow of Thomas Beals,
in the 89th year of her age. Mrs. Beals, whose
maiden name was Field, was born in Madison,
Conn., April 7, 1784. She was a sister of Rev.
David Dudley Field, D.D., of Stockbridge, Mass.,
and of Rev. Timothy Field, first pastor of the Congregational church of Canandaigua. She came to
Canandaigua with her brother, Timothy, in 1800.
In 1805 she was married to Thomas Beals, Esq.,
with whom she lived nearly sixty years, until he
fell asleep. They had eleven children, of whom
only four survive. In 1807 she and her husband
united with the Congregational church, of which
they were ever liberal and faithful supporters. Mrs.
Beals loved the good old ways and kept her house
in the simple and substantial style of the past. She
herself belonged to an age of which she was the
last. With great dignity and courtesy of manner
which repelled too much familiarity, she combined
a sweet and winning grace, which attracted all to
her, so that the youth, while they would almost
involuntarily ' rise up before her,' yet loved to be in
her presence and called her blessed. She possessed
in a rare degree the ornament of a meek and quiet
spirit and lived in an atmosphere of love and peace.
Her home and room were to her children and her

children's children what Jerusalem was to the saints
of old.   There they loved to resort and the saddest
thing in her death is the sundering of that tie which
bound so many generations together.   She never
ceased to take a deep interest in the prosperity of
the beautiful village of which she and her husband
were the pioneers and for which they did so much
and in the church of which she was the oldest member.   Her mind retained its activity to the last and
her heart was warm in sympathy with every good
work.   While she was well informed in all current
events, she most delighted in whatever concerned
the Kingdom.   Her Bible and religious books were
her constant companions and her conversation told
much of her better thoughts, which were in Heaven.
Living so that those who knew her never saw in
her anything but fitness for Heaven, she patiently
awaited the Master's call and went down to her
grave in a full age like a shock of corn fully ripe that
cometh in its season."

I don't think I shall keep a diary any more, only
occasionally jot down things of importance.   Mr.
Noah T. Clarke's brother got possession of my little
diary in some way one day and when he returned it
I found written on the fly-leaf this inscription to
the diary:

" You'd scarce expect a volume of my size
   To hold so much that's beautiful and wise,

And though the heartless world might call me cheap
Yet from my pages some much joy shall reap.
As monstrous oaks from little acorns grow,
And kindly shelter all who toil below,
So my future greatness and the good I do
Shall bless, if not the world, at least a few."

I think I will close my old journal with the mottoes which I find upon an old well-worn writing book which Anna used for jotting down her youthful deeds. On the cover I find inscribed, " Try to be somebody," and on the back of the same book, as if trying to console herself for unexpected achievement which she could not prevent, " Some must be great! "

1880

June 17.—Our dear Anna was married to-day to Mr. Alonzo A. Cummings of Oakland, Cal., and has gone there to live. I am sorry to have her go so far away, but love annihilates space. There is no real separation, except in alienation of spirit, and that can never come—to us.

THE END

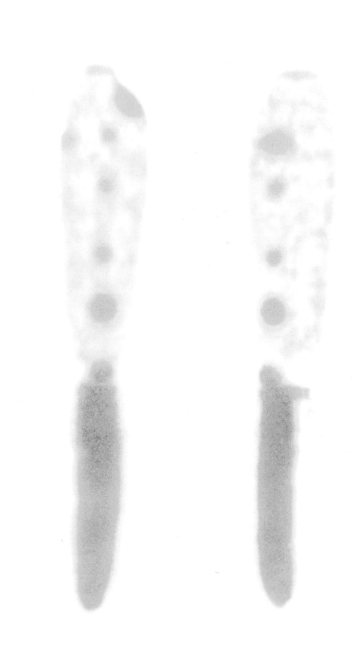